Roger G. Sweeney

Macaws

Everything About Purchase,
Care, Nutrition, Handling, and
Behavior

Filled with Full-color
Photographs

Illustrations by
Michele Earle-Bridges

BARRON'S

2 CONTENTS

UNDERSTANDING MACAWS

Macaws are among the most striking members of the parrot family (Psittacidae). They come from Central and South America and have been widely kept as pets since the beginning of the twentieth century. Some records suggest that Green-winged macaws were being kept as long ago as the turn of the seventeenth century. In the early years of the twentieth century, several macaw species became widely available. Many of the first-recorded breedings stem from this time.

What Is a Macaw?

The macaw group today consists of 17 living species, which are divided into four genera. Although the various species vary greatly in size and coloration, all share some basic physical characteristics. All are known for their long tails, slim bodies, and broad heads, but the large macaws, such as the Scarlet and the Blue and Gold, are instantly recognizable to most people because of their imposing size and vivid coloration. The smaller species, although physically similar, are fairly dull by comparison and are less likely to be recognized at first sight.

Of the four genera of macaws, the genus *Ara* contains 12 of the 17 known living species

Blue and Gold macaws are the most recognizable macaw species in captivity.

seen in captivity, and most of the species usually considered as pet birds fall into this grouping. One species formerly considered to be part of the *Ara* genus has now been separated into its own genus of *Diopsittaca*. This is the Hahn's macaw, which is also a common pet species. Three striking species of large blue macaws form the genus *Andorhynchus*. They are the Hyacinthine, Glaucous, and Lear's macaws. The remaining species is the exceptionally rare Spix's macaw of the monotypic genus *Cyanopsitta,* which is now extinct in the wild with only a small captive population.

Voice and Mimicry

Unlike the Amazon parrots, with whom they often share their range, macaws in their wild

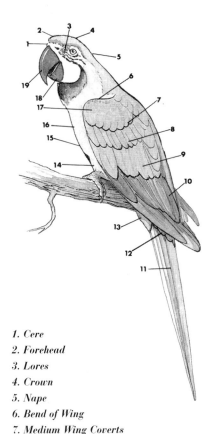

1. Cere
2. Forehead
3. Lores
4. Crown
5. Nape
6. Bend of Wing
7. Medium Wing Coverts
8. Secondary Wing Coverts
9. Secondaries

10. Primaries	15. Abdomen
11. Tail	16. Breast
12. Uppertail Coverts	17. Lesser Wing Coverts
13. Undertail Coverts	18. Lower Mandible
14. Thigh	19. Upper Mandible

Drawing of a macaw that shows the names of various parts of the body. Knowing the correct term to describe a feature can be of great benefit when seeking advice from a veterinarian.

═══ **TIP** ═══

Learning to Speak

A radio or television can keep a bird entertained for many hours when it is alone. Macaws already used to mimicking find this quite stimulating. They may even pick up new words from such listening sessions, though most of the radio dialogue may be spoken too quickly for the bird to absorb it.

state are not great mimics. Vocal expression is mainly used in group situations with birds of their own or similar species. Also unlike Amazons, macaws use only their natural voice, which does not vary greatly in its sound and pitch.

Vocal expression within a group of macaws is not complex. The distinctive cry of the adult macaw, which is instantly recognizable to birds nearby, is used for calling and for recognition. Variations in volume, harshness, and in the call itself are used by macaws to convey several separate recognizable signals, including danger, distress, food, aggression, courtship, recognition of another bird, and affection.

In captivity, however, domestically bred birds will seek to interact with their owners once a relationship of trust has been established. In addition to seeking physical contact, most birds will try to imitate the sounds and movements of their owners. With patience, mimicry can be developed with words being imitated almost perfectly. Once begun, mimicry will continue to increase with a young macaw, as this will prove an excellent way for the bird to attract attention from the owner. Mimicry can also help keep a macaw interested and amused when there is nothing else for it to do.

Handling and Temperament

As strongly suggested throughout this book, only captive-bred macaws should be considered as prospective pets. Wild-caught birds never completely adapt to a household environment and frequently engage in screaming bouts that are certain to test the patience of even the most devoted owner.

When hand-raised, young macaws are generally unafraid of human contact. Nevertheless, a macaw in its first year of life when it is received into the new home will be nervous and will require some time to accept its new owner. Often, hand-raised macaws become attached to the person who has reared them and have had little contact with anyone else. For a young bird, a change in owner usually means a simultaneous move to a new and unfamiliar home. It is not surprising that a young macaw, when first entering its new home environment, can seem totally disoriented and often become shy and nervous. It will need reassurance and patient handling during the first few weeks, but once the bird becomes confident with its new owner and surroundings, it should soon lose all nervousness and regain all of its tameness and inquisitiveness.

Once a trusting relationship has been established between the owner and the macaw, as much time as possible should be spent playing with it. In the wild, macaws are quite affectionate and use much of their resting time to socialize by preening one another. In captivity, the owner of a pet bird is the only source of affection; therefore, the bird will require as much attention as the owner can provide.

Always handle macaws with confidence. It should be remembered that hand-reared macaws never develop a "natural" fear of people. As they grow into adolescence, they can become boisterous, mischievous, and difficult to handle. In this event, the owner should react with confidence at all times to keep the bird's respect. Any sign of nervousness from the owner will be tested by the bird.

Macaws in Nature

In nature, macaws live and behave differently than they do in captivity. This is not really surprising as no captive enclosure could ever come close to recreating their natural lifestyle. Although a wild macaw's home range can cover an extremely large area, macaws are adaptable: In captivity, they adapt to accept

Macaw vocalization is used for recognition of individuals and to convey a number of social messages.

Preening is an important social action between macaws as well as a way to keep feathers in good condition.

the facilities and lifestyle that are available to them. Captive life can be either better or worse than the life the macaw would have in its wild state, but it is certainly not the same. Some aspects of natural behavior are described below, but to completely understand macaws, they must be observed firsthand in their natural setting.

Movement

In captivity macaws are great climbers. They often clamber upside down across the interior roof surface of their enclosure and perform great acrobatics, such as hanging by one toe while spinning around to look at something behind them. In aviaries the majority of the bird's movements involve climbing, especially in a well-branched aviary where the macaws are able to reach every important area of their enclosure from nearby branches. Hence, a pet owner who has never enjoyed the opportunity to observe macaws in nature might assume that much of their movement in the wild is undertaken in the same way. Certainly, a macaw seen walking along the floor in an awkward fashion, all feet and bill, might also lead the observer to

Young hand-reared macaws are dependent upon their owner for affection and companionship.

conclude that macaws are predominantly climbing birds by evolution. Of course, nothing could be further from the truth.

Macaws in their wild state are great flying birds. Once a macaw has taken to the air, the legs neatly folded back, head held out straight, and long wings extended to the fullest, it reveals itself as a powerful and elegant flying bird. Macaws can easily travel many miles while in flight with seemingly little effort; even short distances are flown in preference to climbing. They do climb when necessary within the canopy of a tree in order to reach the particular place of interest to them. In contrast to captive birds that walk or climb short distances between two adjoining branches, wild macaws nearly always fly the distance when in a similar situation.

Habitat and Range

Preferred habitats vary among the different species of macaws, as do distributions and altitudes at which they can be encountered. In general, macaws favor undisturbed, lowland, humid forests, such as those that cover much of South America. Unfortunately, in recent times these areas have been dramatically reduced. Some species can be found at higher altitudes, while others can be found in more open woodlands and on the edges of forests.

The Military macaw, for instance, lives in quite arid regions across much of its range.

Undisturbed forests are essential to the lives of most macaw species. As already mentioned, the natural range for a wild macaw is quite extensive because macaws are strong flyers that will travel widely if necessary to find food. In some species there is evidence of seasonal migration across some parts of their range; thus it is clear that in the long run, populations of macaws cannot survive in isolated parks, but will require large undisturbed areas of forest to thrive.

Food

The foods eaten by different species of macaws vary according to the particular species, the region each inhabits, and what is available seasonally throughout the year. Wild birds have a far higher food requirement than captive birds because they expend far greater amounts of energy throughout the course of the day flying in search of their food. Captive macaws with limited room for exercise and easy access to the food dish, by comparison, need to have their diet regulated to prevent obesity.

Sleeping

Most macaw species sleep or roost communally from dusk until it becomes light enough to fly the following morning. Communal roosting not only reduces the threat from potential predators by increased collective awareness, but also helps in the interaction of pairs.

Pairing

The basic pairing process between macaws does not vary greatly between wild macaws and those bred in captivity, other than the fact that wild macaws usually have more choices of potential mates. In most cases, mate selection is initiated by the female, which shows submission to a male and pulls at his lower mandible, a gesture intended to encourage him to feed her. After pairing has been initiated, the male will then become the dominant bird with behaviors including preening, feeding, and copulation, which in a strong pairing can take place almost daily.

Preening

Preening takes place between a pair of macaws, but also more widely among a flock or social group of macaws. Preening is not only a social interaction that provides reassurance to the birds, but is also essential to feather care and maintenance. Thus, any two birds may begin to preen each other regardless of their relationship within the flock.

Bathing and Showering

Most macaws in the wild and in captivity love bathing in the rain or in a shallow pool of water. In captivity the owner should provide the bird with the opportunity to periodically shower from a light spray or from a container of shallow water provided for this purpose. Bathing or showering is usually followed by prolonged preening, which can entail self-preening as well as group preening.

Breeding

Wild macaws will generally breed and rear young once a year. Average number of eggs and incubation, where known, are described later in this book in the individual descriptions in the species guide (see page 73). The nesting site favored by most species of macaw is a freshly hollowed tree crevice, particularly a palm tree if available. Some macaws have other preferences; for example, the Red-fronted macaw breeds and rears young on a cliff shelf, a practice not common in other species. Young macaws generally fledge and become independent quicker in the wild than is usually the case in captivity; this characteristic is almost certainly due to necessity.

Each year, macaws breed and try to rear their young when the food supply, particularly fruit trees, is most abundant; therefore, it is essential that the first clutch is successful and is reared before the food supply starts to dwindle. Should the first clutch fail for any reason, the pair still has time to rear a second clutch of eggs. Fledging early in the breeding season when food is abundant also helps the young macaws, who must compete with older, more experienced birds for available food. It is not surprising that chicks that hatch late in the breeding season usually have a lower survival rate than those hatched earlier in the breeding season.

Conservation and Aviculture

It cannot be denied that macaws are among the most majestic and the most visually striking of all birds. Their beauty, imposing size, and physical structure combined with their gentle nature and intelligence have given them a special place within aviculture and the pet market for many years. Their success as pets has been aided in recent decades by the development in artificial incubation and hand-rearing techniques, which have produced generations of captive-bred birds that are adaptable, unreserved, and affectionate. Many people, however, believe macaws are even more appreciated when kept as aviary birds in large flights, pointing out that macaws must be seen in flight to truly appreciate them at their best.

With the widespread success that has been achieved in recent decades with the captive breeding of many macaw species in aviculture, the future of these macaw species present in aviculture looks secure. In the wild, however, the numbers of some macaw species are dwindling as habitat destruction increases across Central and South America. If this problem is

What Lies Ahead

The future of many macaws is directly tied to the fate and future management of the forests and other habitats these birds depend on for their survival. The destruction of the South American rain forests is by no means a new problem, but during the last 50 years, the logging industry has pursued an increasingly intense commercialism that has left large expanses of land bare.

As mentioned elsewhere, macaws are great travelers and require extensive forest areas for foraging and nesting. The vast devastation that has already taken place will soon have dramatic effects: The diminished habitat will quickly lead to a reduction in the number of birds that the smaller area can sustain. Moreover, as populations of macaws become isolated from each other by the fractures in their range, other long-term problems will begin to appear, such as increased inbreeding and loss of genetic variability. This chain of events has already started.

The Hyacinthe macaw is endangered in the wild and is the focus of a conservation program.

allowed to continue unchecked, as time passes, perhaps even the status of macaw species that are currently still large, and self-sustaining wild populations, will also deteriorate until these species also become threatened.

As the threats toward the future of wild living macaw populations have become clearer in recent decades, all macaw species have now been listed in either Appendix I or II of the CITES convention to monitor the commercial trade of these species.

It is clear that the properly managed aviculture of as many species of macaw as possible is not only desirable, but also essential to safeguard their future. The responsibilities of the macaw owner can therefore be summarized as follows:

1. All macaws being purchased as pets should be captive bred from a reliable breeder or pet retailer. In the United States, only captive-bred macaws are available as pets; wild macaws are no longer imported. Outside of the United States, the pet owner should not be tempted to purchase a wild-caught macaw, even if the price is significantly lower.

2. Macaws kept singularly as pets should be cared for with as much time and devotion as the owner can provide.

3. Conservation-sensitive species that have not yet become firmly established into a self-sustaining captive population should be kept for breeding and not as pets. Also, every effort must be made to pair these birds to compatible, unrelated partners so they have the opportunity to breed.

Wildlife Legislation Affecting Macaws in Captivity

As many species of macaws have become increasingly endangered in the wild, safeguards have been created to ensure that any birds offered for sale in captivity are indeed legal and captive bred.

CITES: The main legislation that governs the trade of endangered wildlife internationally is the CITES agreement. CITES stands for Convention on International Trade of Endangered Species. All macaw species are included in the CITES appendices so that the trade of

Young Scarlet macaw (**Ara macao**).

wild-caught birds can be properly controlled. In many countries macaws that are included in Appendix I of the CITES agreement require an individual license (see individual species descriptions for CITES listing). In the United States, however, the introduction of the Wild Bird Conservation Act into law from 1992 on has prohibited the import of wild-caught macaws (except under special exemption), therefore replacing the need for any CITES permits to be issued for birds in the United States.

In other words, no license paperwork is required to purchase and own a domestically bred macaw that is within the United States.

A second act of U.S. law governs the movement of endangered animals between different states; this is the Endangered Species Act (ESA). If the species of macaw is listed in the Endangered Species Act, then a permit will be required if the bird is being moved to another state. If the bird is being purchased within the same state as the new owner, then no Endangered Species Act permit is required for the transfer of the bird to its new home.

Once you have decided to purchase a young macaw as a pet, several considerations must be taken into account and some preparation should be undertaken in advance of the macaw's actual arrival at your home.

Housing

The cage or aviary that the macaw will live in should be ready *before* the bird arrives home. Most young macaws probably will not have experienced many dramatic changes in their living environment. To enable the macaw to settle as quickly as possible into its new home, have its cage in move-in condition.

Diet

Before placing the macaw into its new cage for the first time, food and water dishes should already be available inside the cage. These dishes should be placed slightly above perch height within easy reach of the macaw. When a new macaw first arrives at the home, it will probably be nervous and reluctant to experiment with new foods. Therefore, for the first few days after the bird has arrived at a new home, its diet should consist of the same type of food that it had in its former location. Changing the diet or increasing the variety of foods available should not

be undertaken until the macaw has settled in and is feeding well.

Time and Attention

Upon its arrival at the new home, the macaw should receive as much time and attention as you can lavish upon it. In many cases, hand-reared macaws will have been cared for primarily by one person to whom the bird has become closely attached. The loss of that familiar person and the complete change in the living environment can make the macaw feel insecure, which, in turn, could adversely affect its appetite and eventually its health. If routinely there is no one present in the house during the day, you should consider receiving the macaw during a vacation period or even think about taking time off from work to give the bird the attention it will require during its first week in its new home.

Noise

Macaws are among the noisiest of all house pets. If you plan to keep the macaw inside a house or apartment in close proximity to neighbors, you need to seriously question whether keeping such a pet is really feasible. If you are considering a large species, such

Suitable cages for a macaw.

as a Green-winged macaw or a Blue and Gold macaw, it would be prudent to check whether any municipal laws permit or restrict the keeping of macaws as domestic pets before actually acquiring one.

Other Household Occupants

During the first few weeks after its arrival, other large domestic pets, such as dogs or cats, should be kept away from the macaw while it settles in and gains confidence. Young children also need to be supervised when they are near the macaw to keep them from making sudden noises or movements that might alarm the bird.

Choosing a Macaw

Before choosing a macaw, you first have to decide what species to keep. To some extent, this is a matter of personal preference, although the choice will be limited to some degree by external factors, such as which species are readily available, their cost, their size, and space requirements. Macaws that are endangered should not be considered suitable for a pet.

When you have considered the suitability of the different species and decided on the best choice to suit your individual situation, the next step is to select an individual bird. Once a species has been selected, you should find an appropriate breeder of that species or a dealer with a good reputation for selling pet birds.

When selecting an individual bird the first things to look for are signs of good or bad health. These signs are basically the same for adult birds, which are described in detail in the later chapter on health care.

Examine the macaw to ensure that it has a good layer of fat covering the chest and that it does not demonstrate "begging" behavior by bobbing its head and crying to be fed. If the bird exhibits this behavior and the ribs of the chest

A macaw's confidence is always more easily won by offering food treats. This is especially true when dealing with a newly acquired bird.

can be felt, chances are the bird has not been properly weaned and is not a good choice.

After your scrutiny of several individual young macaws to be sure that all appear to be healthy and in good condition, you can then narrow your selection. A confident macaw will usually settle down and be tamed much better than a nervous macaw. When looking at several birds together, try to establish which of those birds remain alert and confident when being viewed, and which of them try to hide or turn away. A macaw that will hold eye contact without appearing to panic is usually the best choice, especially if it will follow the movements of its viewer while still maintaining eye contact. Likewise, when the viewer slowly stretches out a hand toward the cage, a confident bird will show interest rather than nervousness. In general, as long as the bird chosen is captive bred and in good health, you should have few problems taming it.

MACAWS AS PETS

The suitability of keeping a macaw as a pet in most cases depends on whether you really do have the time, space, and financial resources required to provide for all of the bird's needs. As stated throughout this book, only captive-bred birds should be considered as pets, and it is advantageous when possible for the new owner to purchase the macaw directly from the breeder who raised the bird.

Acclimatization and Quarantine

Acclimatization is a term that relates to helping a bird adjust to a significant change of the environment in which it is kept, usually a significant change in temperature. Acclimatization is important when caring for any new bird, even one that has been domestically bred in the same state or town as the new owner. Most young macaws bred to be pets have been hand-raised and have therefore grown up in an artificial indoor environment. Macaws reared in such a protected environment can be very susceptible to drafts, cold, or excessive heat. Therefore, care should be taken to ensure that the bird is comfortable and warm enough in its new home.

If the new pet is to be kept in an outdoor aviary, its introduction to the aviary should be

With the proper care and handling, macaws can make exceptionally good pets.

done very carefully, particularly in regions where the weather can be unpredictable. A gradual approach is always prudent. You can start by placing the bird in the aviary during daylight hours and bringing it inside at night until you are sure that the bird is fully adjusted to the weather conditions and is comfortable.

Quarantine is a term usually used to describe the period of isolation that wild-caught birds are held in to ensure that they are not carrying disease; for all parrot species this is set at 45 days. In a strict quarantine the air supply should be separate from that of established birds and you should make sure that separate feeding bowls, cleaning equipment, and even the clothes you wear to care for the birds in quarantine are kept separate from the same items you would use and wear when caring for established pet birds.

Although captive-bred macaws are unlikely to carry the same diseases that can affect parrots in the wild, there are some illnesses that a young, or domestically bred macaw can be prone to, particularly if it has lived in a pet shop environment and has mixed with a variety of other pet birds. Quarantine of any new bird, therefore, should be considered if you already keep other pet parrots in your home. The new bird should be placed in a separate room and monitored for a period of 45 days and should be closely observed for any signs of poor health prior to contact with other pet birds already living in your home. This quarantine period will serve two main purposes:

✔ to allow the new bird a period to gain confidence and build a bond to the new owner, and

✔ to protect the established pet parrots from any health problems that the new bird might be suffering from.

Handling and Restraint

Macaws are among the largest of parrots and it is important for you to be confident in handling and restraining the macaw if required.

When holding a macaw, position one hand around the back of the bird's head, thereby securing either side of the lower mandible. With the other hand, secure the wings and legs.

Larger macaw species have the potential to deliver painful and physically damaging bites—even the bite from one of the smaller species can be painful and unpleasant. With a young macaw being purchased as a pet bird, you will be looking to establish a relationship based on trust, so physical restraint of the bird should not be practiced unless absolutely necessary for a health-related problem. This often can be done with the assistance of a veterinarian who is experienced in handling large parrots.

Macaws are most easily restrained once they are on the floor.

✔ You can cover the bird with either a net or a large towel and then carefully seize it.

✔ In holding a macaw, place the first hand around the back of the head with your thumb and index finger reaching around to the sides of the macaw's lower mandible.

✔ With the second hand, support the main part of the macaw's weight, holding the legs and wings at the same time to prevent the bird from struggling.

TIP

Handling Macaws

Handling macaws can be dangerous. If you have any doubt, seek assistance from an experienced person or your veterinarian before attempting to touch or restrain a large macaw.

Transporting Macaws

Travel boxes that are intended for use in transporting large macaws need to be extremely sturdy to withstand the attentions of a macaw's beak. There is a wide range of commercially produced travel boxes for dogs, cats, and other

Trimming of the toenails should always be done with care to avoid cutting into the quick.

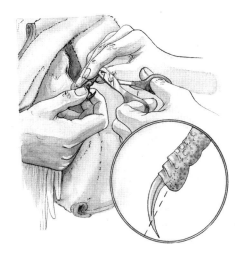

domestic animals that are very suitable for use in transporting a macaw, as long as they are sturdy enough and a few alterations can be made.

Perches: If the macaw is going to remain in the carrying box for a long period of time, a wooden perch should be secured inside the box to prevent its feet from cramping, which occurs if the bird is left to stand on a flat floor surface. The perch should be fixed across the width of the box at about one third of the height of the box. This should allow sufficient head clearance so the macaw can comfortably sit erect.

Ventilation: Most domestic animal-carrying boxes have a grill type or large ventilation holes on the sides; this allows you to secure food and water dishes inside the travel box.

One final point to remember when transporting more than one macaw is that each macaw should be housed individually while being moved in order to avoid fighting from occuring while the birds are stressed and nervous.

Beak and Toenail Trimming

As with all parrots, the beak and toenails of a macaw grow continuously throughout the bird's life. In the wild, macaws wear down their bills by scraping and chewing on tree branches. Their toenails are naturally worn down by daily abrasion against tree branches. Captive macaws need to have their cages furnished with natural tree branches, which must be replaced with fresh material as often as possible. The macaw should also be provided with additional pieces of wood, small enough so the bird can hold them in its foot while being chewed. Even with

the provision of fresh chewing material on a regular basis, it may still be necessary to occasionally trim either the beak or toenails.

Beak Trimming

Trimming the beak of a macaw can be quite easily done if you are confident and experienced in handling large parrots. Such a procedure may require two persons, as the macaw will have to be restrained for the trimming to be carried out safely. Trim only a small amount of the bill and allow the macaw to correct the remainder by the providing fresh chewing wood. Cases of extremely overgrown bills should be referred to an experienced avian veterinarian. Great care should be taken to ensure that the macaw's tongue is always kept away from the trimming instrument. If you are not confident in handling a large macaw, you should take it to an avian veterinarian.

Toenail Trimming

Toenail trimming is a more common procedure than bill trimming. Care should be taken not to

Stress and Health

Many health problems can be carried by a young macaw, but only become obvious once the young bird is subject to increased stress. Being moved into a new home with unfamiliar surroundings and people can be stressful and trigger illness.

trim toenails too heavily. Remember that as the toenail grows longer, so does the vein that runs inside of it. Therefore, long-neglected toenails should not be cut back too severely as care must be taken when trimming to not cut into the vein and cause bleeding. (Often, the vein can actually be seen when viewed against sunlight.) After trimming, provide the macaw with freshly cut

natural tree branches as cage perches to give it the opportunity to further wear down its toenails. When cutting toenails, always hold the clippers at an angle to ensure that the upper surface is slightly longer than the lower surface of the nail. This angle conforms to the natural shape of the nail and helps the bird wear down any rough edges created by the trimming.

Feather Clipping

Feather clipping is the procedure of cutting the flight feathers to reduce the bird's flying ability. This can be undertaken in either just one wing, or in both wings. When only one wing is trimmed, the bird will be very unbalanced when it tries to fly and will quickly land on the floor. This technique is often used in public areas such as zoos to prevent birds from potentially having access to the public. On the other hand, when both of the wings are trimmed, the bird will have very limited but more balanced flying ability, being able to fly downward slightly further and to a safer landing.

For domestic pet situations it is usually recommended that both of the wings be trimmed so that the macaw can land more safely, particularly if the macaw is still young and learning. The idea of trimming the wings of a macaw is to allow more freedom for the bird to venture outside of its cage without the risk of it flying away. Also, in the case of a young pet macaw becoming used to a new household environment, feather clipping can reduce the potential for accidents such as flying into a

A macaw needs plenty of wood to chew. Chewing prevents the beak from becoming too long.

A Buffon's macaw accepts a food treat from the hand.

window, furniture, and other household objects. Young macaws, if handled regularly from an early age, can have their feathers clipped without the need to restrain them. You can accustom the macaw to this procedure by extending its wing from time to time during routine handling. Each feather clipped should be cut just below the level of the wing covert feather.

The bird's flight feathers are divided into primary feathers (on the outer edge of the wing) and secondary feathers (on the inner side of the wing). The primary flight feathers are most important when the bird flies, so feather clipping should concentrate upon the primaries. Care should be taken when clipping flight feathers to avoid cutting young feathers (called *blood feathers*) that are still growing. Because they are still growing, blood feathers have a living vein inside them that will bleed when cut.

Identification Marking

Marking macaws for the purpose of correct identification is of increased importance for many reasons:

• To deter thefts

• To prevent mistakes in identification when birds are paired or mixed together

• To aid better record keeping of captive populations (perhaps the most important of these reasons).

Various marking techniques can be used to identify individual macaws, the most common of which are described as follows.

Leg Bands

Leg bands are either "open" or "closed" in design. Both types are made from strong metal (for macaws, stainless steel leg bands are recommended), and have an easy-to-read individual identification code, made up from a combination of letters and numbers, punched into the ring. Both types of leg bands are available in different sizes to meet the different size and strength requirements of the various macaw species. Open leg bands can be fitted to an adult bird at any stage of its life. They can be obtained in a "C" shape, which is then closed onto the leg of the macaw by a special pair of applicator pliers. Closed leg bands are solid rings that can be fitted to the leg of a macaw only at a young age (normally 28–34 days of age). If a correctly sized closed leg band is present on the leg of a macaw, it is strong evidence that the macaw was domestically bred in captivity. Leg bands are easy to use as an identification method and are usually easy to check and read.

Microchip Implants

The use of microchip implants as a form of identification has increased in recent years, particularly in countries where the potential for theft of expensive parrots is a concern. One problem with external marking, such as the use of leg bands, is that they can potentially be removed by a thief, whereas a microchip implant is a permanent form of identification that is extremely difficult to remove once placed into a macaw. The implanting of an identification microchip is a veterinary procedure, and should be carried out only by a qualified veterinarian. The microchip is most commonly inserted into the breast muscle of the bird, although sometimes an area of loose skin, such as the neck or under the wing, can be selected instead. The microchip has a unique code, usually made up from a combination of numbers and letters, which can be picked up and read by a scanner passed over the macaw's body.

Temporary Marking Methods

Sometimes, even though the macaw might already have a permanent form of identification as described above, the owner may wish to use a short-term form of marking the bird that is much more visually striking. The most common reason why the owner of a macaw would wish to do this would be to more easily identify each bird at a distance when a number of macaws are placed together in a communal situation. Placing the birds in a communal situation can be done either for natural mate selection pairing to take place or simply to provide the macaws with social interaction outside of the breeding season. The use of a safe spray marker (recommended by your veterinarian) is one easy way to place individual marks on each macaw, although care should be taken when applying the spray to avoid the face of the bird.

Another common short-term marking technique used for macaws is selective trimming of tail fathers. The long tail feathers of macaws are quite visible and so selective trimming of either the side or central tail feathers can make an individual macaw easily recognizable from some distance away.

Taming and Training

Once the macaw has settled into its new surroundings and is eating well, you can then begin to work on building a closer relationship with the bird. Macaws are intelligent birds, and with time and patience the bird can become tame and affectionate toward the owner, as well as having the potential to mimic speech.

Providing that the aviculturist has obtained a young hand-reared macaw, it is likely that the bird is already tame, but it may be nervous and disoriented having just arrived in new and unfamiliar surroundings. In the first few days after the parrot's arrival, you need to reassure the bird so that it will begin to build up a base of confidence in you and the new home environment. Once the young macaw has gained confidence, it will become extremely willing to seek your attention and affection.

Instilling Confidence

The first step in reassuring a young macaw is to spend time sitting close by. This allows the macaw to become used to the sight of you and the sound of your voice. Attempts to touch the bird should not be rushed if it appears to be nervous. You should wait until the bird clearly demonstrates that it wants closer contact. In the first few days, your presence sitting next to the bird cage can make the macaw a little nervous; but it's important that the young bird not be isolated during this period. It is absolutely essential that the bird have someone it can relate to as soon as possible in the new home environment. This interaction with you will help the bird settle more easily into its new home. Soon after the macaw has settled, it will begin to display a confident interest in your presence.

Offering Food Treats

The macaw can be encouraged to seek closer contact with you if its favorite food items are offered by your hand, which it usually soon accepts. To begin with, the food treat can be placed in the cage bars for the macaw to accept, then in your outstretched hand. Once the parrot is confident enough to accept food from your hand, it will soon also allow you to touch its chest and also the back of the neck and head to gently scratch it.

Bringing the Bird Outside the Cage

When the bird develops greater confidence and interest in the room surroundings, you can start to bring it outside of the cage every day. However, the wing feathers should be trimmed to prevent the bird from flying into a window or other obstacle. The cage door can be left open. Once the bird is confident, it will climb through the door and onto the top of the cage. If the cage is not already equipped with a perch on the cage roof, you should secure a branch so that the parrot can comfortably perch on top of the cage for a while. These extended periods of freedom from the cage should be allowed only while you are close by to keep an eye on the macaw to prevent accidents.

Stepping Up

The macaw should react confidently to the freedom from the cage and demonstrate an increased interest in following you around the room. You can now begin to offer your hand and lower arm toward the macaw to encourage it to step up onto you. For the young macaw to step off the cage and onto your arm it must have confidence in the firmness and stability of the arm, so your movements should

A Green-winged macaw chews a cut branch and attacks a block of wood as chewing material.

be sure and without hesitation. Often the macaw can be encouraged to step onto the arm for the first time by offering a food treat, which it can reach only by stepping up onto your arm. This may require some patience, but soon the macaw will have the confidence to trust the stability of your arm. The confidence of the young macaw can also be encouraged by using a verbal command or signal, such as the words *"Step up!"* If you bring your arm up slowly and without hesitation toward the macaw at the same time the *"Step up!"* voice signal is used, then the macaw will quickly learn that you are asking it to climb onto the arm and respond to this request with confidence. Once the macaw has become used to perching on your arm, it will usually enjoy the closer contact with you and will enthusiastically go to your arm whenever it is offered.

Stages of Growth

The macaw will soon begin to feel like a member of the family. Tame macaws will pass

A young Military macaw is comfortable sitting on the owner's hand.

Above: A Scarlet macaw enjoys playing with a wooden toy.

Right: A Green-winged macaw and a Hyacinthe macaw delight in playing with a commercial parrot toy.

through an adolescent stage (usually between 18 and 36 months of age) and you will have to take care not to let the macaw become too demanding as it will try to assert its wishes for your attention. Often, if a macaw feels neglected it will whistle, rattle its food dishes, or even screech until it gets its own way. You should continue to spend quality time with the pet macaw consistently each day while it passes through this difficult stage, but bad behavior, such as screeching or even biting, should not be tolerated.

If the macaw is too boisterous when handled, it should be returned to the cage until later in the day when it is calmer and can be more easily handled.

Aggressive behavior: If the macaw tries to bite, you should state "*No!*" in a loud and firm voice and you should simply withdraw from the area of the cage until the bird is less excited. If aggressive behavior is allowed to develop and is accepted by the owner, it can become an increasing problem as the macaw gets older. All adolescent macaws will pass through some bouts of bad behavior, but following the basic advice given here and using common sense, the macaw should have grown out of most patterns of bad behavior after 36 months of age. There is a variety of books dealing specifically with the subject of behavioral problems in pet birds; you can consult them if you become concerned.

CHECKLIST

Entertaining a Pet Macaw

1. Regular supplies of fresh chewing wood (with leaves).
2. Regular excursions from the cage.
3. Plenty of quality time between you and your pet.
4. Pinecones (must be cleaned first).
5. Wooden kitchen spoons.
6. Cardboard roll inside of paper towels or toilet paper.
7. Other safe (nontoxic), old wooden or cardboard chewable items.
8. Television.
9. Radio.
10. Selection of commercial macaw toys as seen in pet magazines.

In cases where you become nervous about handling the macaw because of problematic behavior, then advice should be sought from an experienced macaw breeder, avian veterinarian, or bird behavioral specialist who can work with you to ensure that the macaw's behavior is properly responded to and that you can confidently handle and train the macaw through this difficult age period.

Mimicking

Macaws can be good at mimicking sounds and words. If you are patient, macaws can be taught to mimic words and phrases. When trying to teach the macaw to mimic, remember that its attention span is short. Short and frequent lessons work much more effectively than trying to spend an hour at a time repeating phrases to the bird. The macaw will be most alert when it is first approached, but its attention starts to diminish after five minutes or so. Giving the macaw a food reward whenever a teaching session takes place creates a sense of anticipation that will greatly increase the level of the bird's attention each time you approach and begin to repeat words to the bird.

The word *"Hello"* is often the first word tried when teaching a bird to mimic. The word should be stated clearly and slowly; exaggerating the two syllables: *"Hell-o."* Again, the lesson should be short, about five minutes long, and a food treat offered at the end of each session. The bird can be given as many short lessons in a day as you can devote to this task. After the macaw has begun to mimic the first word, additional words can be taught in the same way. Using the first word learned is important in helping the macaw understand that you are encouraging it to mimic. The first word will help trigger the macaw into mimicking the new words along with the one it has already learned.

Keeping a Pet Macaw Entertained

How to keep a pet macaw entertained during the periods that it will have to be confined alone inside its cage is an important consideration. The successful solution can vary greatly depending upon the personality differences between individual birds.

Chewing Material

All macaws love to chew and this activity is an obvious answer to boredom. Chewing material is one of the best occupational materials that can be regularly provided for the bird.

✔ Fresh branches complete with leaves and bark should be given to the macaw on a regular basis. These branches should be replaced with new chewing material as soon as the previous branches have become either completely broken down by chewing or have become hard and dry.

✔ Natural fiber ropes can also be useful when suspended in the cage or aviary. The bird can either hang on them or chew them. Only natural fiber ropes should be used—not artificial fiber. The reason: Natural fiber rope will break easily when the macaw chews on it, thereby presenting less risk of entanglement.

✔ All ropes used should be regularly inspected and replaced when they become frayed or worn.

Toys

There are a number of commercially produced occupational toys now being manufactured for parrots and advertised in avicultural and pet care magazines. Some of these products work better than others and each macaw has its own likes and dislikes. You may wish to try some of these products to see if any of them are enjoyed by the macaw. Always check that the toy you purchase is safe for large parrots. Remember that macaws have strong bills and enjoy objects that they can grind in their bill or that can be manipulated in the bill. Other potential toys may already be available in your home and garden, such as old wooden cooking spoons, empty toilet paper rolls, pinecones, and leafy twigs. Often these items can be combined with a natural fiber rope to create a hanging mixture of interesting and chewable items for the bird to explore and dissemble. You are encouraged to be as creative as possible in designing your own toys and games for the macaw, as long as all items used are safe (nontoxic) and that there is no risk of a toy entangling the macaw or being dangerous if swallowed.

Visual and Acoustic Stimulants

Visual and acoustic stimulants are also worth consideration. Leaving a television set or a radio playing can provide mental stimulation to a bird that is alone in the house. Macaws that have already demonstrated their ability to mimic sounds and words can derive some entertainment from listening to the radio, which may also help expand their vocabulary. Colorful and lively television programs usually catch the macaw's attention; cartoons and other types of programs for young children may be watched by the macaw with more interest than other slower and less lively daytime shows. All of these ideas should be tried by you in an effort to find the best way to provide entertainment for your bird. Many other new ideas can usually be found by reading some of the many pet bird magazines that are available and looking at new products being advertised. The names and addresses of many suitable magazines are included in Information, page 92.

HOUSING

Hand-reared macaws are highly intelligent and, when kept as pets, can be extremely affectionate companions. On the other hand, they also can be extremely destructive and noisy, so the decision to keep a macaw as a pet in your home should be carefully thought out.

Pet Macaws Inside the Home

Selecting the most appropriate room within the home for the macaw to live in is perhaps the first consideration. The bird requires a warm, draft-free site that is not continually exposed to direct sunlight from a window. Placing the macaw's cage near a window may seem like a good idea, but it may prove to be a mistake. Although this location will provide the macaw with something to watch when there is no one in the house, problems can ensue. The macaw can overheat if the window receives direct sunlight, or become susceptible to colds or chills if the window has even the slightest draft. To help create a feeling of security in the macaw's new surroundings, its cage should be located against a wall in a well-lit area.

Noise

Hand-reared birds are normally happiest when they are placed within watching distance

A Scarlet macaw enjoys eating a nut.

of the family's activity and are constantly able to see things happening. Keep in mind, however, that although they enjoy being housed in active, well-occupied rooms, such birds may become frustrated and noisy if they feel they are being neglected or ignored. Remember that the noise created by the macaw can be bothersome not only to you but also to any neighbors that live nearby. The possibility of the noise provoking complaints from neighbors should be seriously considered. Keeping a young macaw is a long-term commitment. That bird may well live in your house for more than 50 years. What may start out as minor irritations with neighbors over noise can, over time, build into major disputes.

Destructiveness

The potential destructiveness of macaws is another point that must not be underestimated. Hand-reared macaws are highly inquisitive and playful. As pets, their activity each day is wholly centered on playing with their owner or with toys. Also, a pet macaw will appreciate the opportunity to wander outside of its cage to find something new that interests it. Such excursions outside of the cage, although of great importance to your bird's happiness, should always be supervised; otherwise, the destructive interest in your household objects can have expensive consequences. Macaws are counted among the most powerful "chewers" in the parrot family. In the time that it takes for you to leave the room to answer the telephone or make a cup of coffee, a macaw at liberty can dismember a table, a chair, or anything else that may have attracted its attention.

Occupational Needs

The macaw's occupational needs also should be considered and attempts must be made to satisfy its curious and spirited nature. This is especially true when a macaw is left alone in a house for much of the day while the family is at work or school. Such a macaw will have to be confined to a cage to prevent damage to the household furniture and to prevent injuries to the bird. Every effort should be made, however, to provide the bird with things to do until you return and can spend time with it. Give your macaw plenty of large nuts and other occupational foods such as corn on the cob that it can enjoy biting or picking with its bill as it eats. Providing regular natural branches and pieces of chewing wood (as described earlier) will not only keep your bird's bill and toenails trimmed to a suitable length but will stave off boredom as well. As previously mentioned, many people like to leave a radio or television on near the cage. This has proved successful in keeping many pet macaws entertained, and has also helped increase the mimicking ability of some macaws.

Access to Water

One last point needs to be mentioned because it has particular relevance to the welfare of a macaw kept as a house pet. Whereas macaws housed in outside aviaries are able to shower in the rain, or have a bathing area available to them, birds that are kept inside the house are deprived of these benefits. For this reason, particularly during hot and dry summer months, be sure to provide your macaw with bathing water on a regular basis. Or, spray your bird with a mister. Access to water is very important because when a bird is hot and sticky it resorts to excessive preening, which may leave its feathers too dry and without natural oils. Such plumage problems must be avoided, because once developed, they can become extremely difficult to reverse.

After considering the bird's requirements and adverse tendencies you can now look at how to provide suitable accommodation for your macaw. This is a question that must be considered well in advance of purchasing a macaw because the appropriate housing for it must be in place prior to the bird's arrival. Several types of housing are available for the macaw owner. These fall into two main categories: indoor pet cages and stands or outdoor garden cages/aviaries.

Indoor Cages and Stands

When considering indoor accommodations for a pet macaw, the primary concern usually revolves around which piece of equipment to use—a cage or a stand. The best answer, not surprisingly, is a combination of the two. The cage is the main unit for keeping the macaw inside the house since, as already mentioned, it would be foolish to allow such a destructive pet unlimited freedom at all times; you must protect not only your household articles but the safety of the macaw as well.

Size

The cage for a large macaw should ideally be no smaller than 31.5 inches long by 31.5 inches wide by 71 inches high (80 cm × 80 cm × 180 cm). Smaller species of macaw can live in comparatively smaller cages. As a guide, the pet macaw should be able to sit on the perches provided and have sufficient head room, while at the same time the tail feathers should not touch the floor of the cage. Also, the bird should be able to stretch its wings without being too confined by the width of the cage. Macaw cages will occupy a large space within the house, so some advanced thought needs to be exercised in deciding on its best placement.

Perches

Most owners generally like to allow their macaw as much freedom as possible when there are people in the house who can keep an eye on it. It is not convenient to carry the macaw around the house on your arm all the time. If the cage door is left open, often the macaw will be content to climb out the door and up to the top of its cage where it can watch all that is going on around it.

But the top of the cage is not always the most comfortable surface for the macaw to perch on because of the size and spacing of the cage bars. As a result, the bird can become restless and start to wander away. Providing the bird with a more comfortable perch, either attached to the top of the cage or by a freestanding one separate from the cage, will allow the bird to perch comfortably for long periods of time when it is outside of the cage confines.

The use of a separate stand, upon which the macaw can perch once it's outside the cage, has the advantage of maneuverability. You can position it wherever the family is concentrated, thus making the bird feel more a part of the family's activities without the need to carry it continually or worry about damage caused by the bird wandering about on its own.

As discussed earlier, it is better if the perches within the cage are made from freshly cut branches that are approximately 2 to 3 inches (5 cm–8 cm) in diameter. These will provide the rough texture the bird needs for a better grip; the variable width and size of natural branches will also help to prevent cramps, from which the bird can suffer if all the perches provided are of a uniform size and an unsuitable shape for the macaw in question.

Potential Hazards Inside the Home

At this point it is well worth noting in more detail some of the dangers that a young pet macaw might encounter in the household environment. Some of the most common dangers are described below.

Electric outlets and wires: Any access to live electrical sockets and wiring can present the risk of potential electrical shocks for the macaw. The strong bill of a pet macaw can quickly slice through wiring or dismantle electrical outlets. Any such occurrence will almost certainly lead to the death of the macaw.

Paint: Paint can either be water-based (such as latex) or petroleum hydrocarbon-based (such as enamels and oil paints). Water-based paints are generally considered safe for pet birds, although the fumes from fresh paint may

Corn-on-the-cob makes a good occupational food that can keep a macaw entertained as well as fed.

irritate the bird's eyes. The fumes from hydro-carbon-based paints are, however, much more directly harmful to the bird's health. A pet macaw should never be near the area where such paint is being used. Also, care should be taken that the bird does not get into the habit of scraping off paint from metal surfaces; this dried paint may contain lead and can be toxic to the bird. Any paint used to prevent rust on the metal work of the macaw's cage should always be checked to ensure that it is lead free and nontoxic.

Water traps: Water traps where a macaw could become stuck are an uncommon but real risk in the home, particularly if the pet macaw has limited flight ability. For example, if a macaw were to land awkwardly in a toilet, accidental drowning might occur.

PVC pipes: PVC pipes can be a hazard if the macaw has the opportunity to chew them. Pet macaws should be kept away from areas of exposed pipes.

New carpets: New carpets and padding can sometimes release toxic fumes when first laid. Care should be taken when new carpets are installed. If necessary, the pet macaw should be housed away from these areas.

Cupboards, shelves, and other fabricated furnishings: These may be made of materials that have been constructed using adhesives that can contain toxic additives (such as formaldehyde).

Teflon cooking utensils: When heated, cooking utensils made from Teflon can produce

CHECKLIST

Household Dangers
1. Access to electric wires and outlets.
2. Fumes from fresh paint.
3. Access to potential water traps.
4. Access to PVC pipes.
5. Fumes from new carpets and padding.
6. Fumes from heated Teflon cookware.
7. Wooden furniture treated with toxic preservatives or glues.
8. Unseen heat from the stove or other electrical devices.
9. Access to toxic houseplants.
10. Access to windows and mirrors that the bird might fly into.

Macaws love to chew and can be destructive if they get hold of household items.

fumes that are extremely toxic to pet birds. These cooking items should not be used in close proximity to any pet birds.

Unseen heat traps: If the macaw has access to the kitchen, and particularly if it has limited flying ability, care should be taken with the electric rings of the stove or other heated appliances. These can burn or scald a pet macaw that cannot visually detect the heat of an object.

Houseplants: Some houseplants, and also outdoor plants, can be toxic if they are ingested by a pet macaw. Examples of toxic plants often encountered in the home include pointsettia, mistletoe, and holly (at Christmas time), hydrangea, and hyacinth. Outdoor plants that are toxic to macaws include philodendron, boxwood, hemlock, morning glory, narcissus, and daffodil.

Glass windows and mirrors: If the macaw has limited ability to fly, remember that it will not recognize a glass window as a solid barrier. Flying into windows is a common accident for pet birds, particularly since the view outside is usually brighter and more attractive to the macaw than the indoor room environment.

Outdoor Cages and Aviaries

Materials

In purchasing or building an aviary for macaws, the first consideration is that it should be constructed with materials that will stand up to both the natural elements and the powerful bill of the macaw. Most outdoor aviaries used in aviculture consist of a wooden frame, but this is unsuitable for macaws because they would soon chew and destroy all the exposed wood accessible to them. Macaw aviaries usually have a structural framework constructed from either brick or metal.

Size of Cover

Next you need to select the size of the wire mesh needed to cover the aviary. Although this is a matter of personal preference, with large-bodied parrots such as macaws, large-gauge wire can be used. More visually attractive than smaller-gauge wire, strong large-gauge wire can provide an easy-to-climb surface for the macaw. However, also remember that part of the purpose of the wire mesh is not only to keep the macaw inside, but also to prevent access into the cage from small native birds and vermin, both of which can contaminate the aviary and endanger the health of the macaw.

Positioning

The positioning of the aviary depends to a great extent on the size and shape of the land available. I have always preferred for outdoor aviaries to have at least one section facing south to give the birds full advantage of the sun throughout the day. This is particularly important in cool climates where the first warm rays of the sun are eagerly appreciated by the waking birds in the early morning hours. The aviary structure must be designed to provide the macaw with shelter against the excesses of sun, rain, and particularly wind. To accomplish this the back wall of the aviary should be solid and the rear 6.5 feet (2 m) of the roof and both sidewalls should also be covered.

Floors

Every possible step must be taken to prevent rodents and other vermin from digging into the aviary. This can be achieved by excavating a layer of the floor within the aviary structure and covering it with concrete, with drainage provided by side holes that must also be covered by wire mesh. Alternatively, a layer of wire mesh can cover the floor instead of concrete. In the latter case, an additional layer of floor medium will be required over the top of the wire mesh.

The floor medium to be used on the base of the aviary is a matter of personal choice. Grass, sand, gravel, paving stones, or a combination are commonly used. Whichever one is used, the owner should ensure that the aviary is easy to clean on a daily basis. If grass is used make sure that periodic trimming of the grass can be easily undertaken without undue stress to the bird—which will have to be accommodated elsewhere during the trimming for safety reasons. Once the pet macaw has settled into the aviary and has chosen its preferred branches to rest on, an area underneath the preferred branches can be made easier to clean by either placing a paving stone or an area of sand to facilitate easier removal of accumulated feces.

Internal Furnishings

After the main construction of the aviary has been completed, you will need to think about the placement of internal furnishings. These include the nest box, receptacles for both food and water, and branches to provide perching.

Nest box: Because in most cases the back of the aviary is sheltered, this is the most advantageous site for a nest box to be positioned. Place the box high up in the back corner with the entrance hole looking out across the aviary.

Food and water dishes: The sheltered area of the aviary is also the most suitable site for the food and water dishes. Food that is left out in the open can become waterlogged in the rain or dry in the sun. Also, the food supply must be protected from contamination by the excretion of native birds that may roost above the aviary. Food dishes can be safely placed towards the back of the aviary on a shelf that has a raised lip along its edges to prevent the dishes from being knocked off easily by the birds. Or, the dishes can be secured into place by means of metal frames. Your macaws will need water for drinking and, during hot weather, also for bathing. Locate the water containers in a protected and easily accessible site because they require daily cleaning and replenishment. Water that is allowed to stand for too long in warm weather can become stale or even be contaminated by native vermin.

Perching: Perching is one of the most important considerations for the aviary. If the aviary inhabitants are to have easy access to food and water, as well as the nesting site, the placement of these features has to be determined before the perching is arranged.

Security

A final consideration is the security of the macaw in an outside aviary. Parrots and particularly macaws are expensive pets and can be targets for theft. Picking a secure location for the aviary is of paramount importance. Macaws are generally loud birds and become even louder when disturbed by unexpected intruders. If the aviary is located near the owner's house, their cries can alert anyone inside, especially if the bird is heard at an unusual time of the night when they should be at roost. Additionally, although aviaries can never be completely theft-proof, the use of a

Above: Natural branches of uneven shape help to exercise the macaw's feet.
Top right: A Military macaw relishes chewing on wooden branches.
Bottom right: A Hyacinthe macaw enjoys being in an outdoor cage.

Opposite page.
Top left: Perching stands can allow the macaw to come out from the cage, while still keeping it a safe distance from household dangers.
Top right: A Blue and Gold macaw is brought out from its cage.
Bottom left: Perching stands can be enhanced with toys and chewing wood to keep the macaw entertained.
Bottom right: Yellow-collared macaws in outdoor aviary.

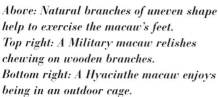

strong structure, heavy-gauge wire mesh, and padlocks on the doors are helpful. Physical restraints at least make it difficult for any potential thieves to enter the aviary and can delay them long enough for someone in the house to become aroused by the disturbance.

Indoor Suspended Cages

The growing use of suspended cages for keeping and breeding captive macaws has proved successful in recent years, although the size of cage needed to adequately house a pair of large macaws is much larger than that of most commercially available cages. Suspended cages basically have an all-wire construction. As their name implies, they are suspended above the floor to leave the area underneath the cage clear for easy cleaning; the bottom panels of the cage are also made of wire to allow excess food and feces to fall through to the floor and out of the macaws' reach to eliminate the health risks that feces and spoiled food represent to them.

Securing your birds' food dishes in place is especially important in this type of cage because if these containers are allowed to overturn all the food will pass out of the cage. Revolving food trays, however, are now widely available for use with these cages. A unique advantage of using these trays is that they allow replenishment of the food and water supply without the need to actually enter the cage itself. Free of this disturbance, the birds seem to gain an increased sense of security soon after they become accustomed to their new accommodation.

As with any type of accommodation, an important point to remember in locating the suspended cage is that macaws are at their happiest when they are perching high above the heads of their keepers and looking down on them. Suspending the cage with its base approximately 5 feet (1.5 m) above the ground will therefore allow you enough room underneath the cage for easy cleaning and maintenance, as well as give your macaw the high perch it prefers, provided, of course, that the cage is of appropriate size.

The size of the suspended cage is determined by the size and species of macaw that is to be housed within it. For most of the large species the minimum dimensions required are 13 feet (4 m) in length by 6$\frac{1}{2}$ feet (2 m) in both width and height. Smaller macaws, such as the Severe, Noble, or Yellow-collared need a cage 10 feet (3 m) long by 5 feet (1.5 m) wide by 6$\frac{1}{2}$ feet (2 m) high (the same height is necessary to also give the smaller macaws a high perch).

Perching should be provided across the width of and at about half-way up the suspended cage in at least three places (one of which must be within easy access to food and water dishes). This arrangement should provide the bird with sufficient perches and also leave it enough open space to jump or fly from perch to perch. For toenail and bill maintenance, perching can be supplemented with extra pieces of wood that can be either placed on the floor of the cage or attached to its sides.

Nest boxes for suspended cages are usually placed outside the cage and a hole is cut in the cage wires to provide access to the box. An inspection flap can be added to one side of the nest box to permit examination of nest contents without the need to enter the cage itself and disrupt the birds.

It is always best to place the nest box toward the back of the aviary, where it will be least disturbed. Some people have experimented with L-shaped cages which are positioned with the L bend at the back of the aviary; they have found great success by blocking off the sides of the bend and locating the nest box in this area. Again, the increased security that this site seems to give the birds is generally reflected in the improved breeding results. Additionally, the L bend gives the birds a place to retreat out of sight without their having to use the nest box itself for this purpose.

There are therefore many advantages to using suspended cages for breeding macaws. Keep in mind, however, that this type of cage is intended for breeding birds and is not considered suitable for pet birds. The purpose of a suspended cage is to create a secure and undisturbed environment to make breeding birds more confident. But such an environment would deprive hand-reared pet birds of the human contact and attention they actively seek. A pet bird housed in this type of cage needs to be provided with a mate to which it can devote its time and attention.

Wooden Branches for Perches and Chewing

Providing the macaw with a regular supply of fresh branches for perches and also for chewing material is of great importance. Natural branches of varying size will help keep the macaw's feet healthy and exercised, preventing cramps or the development of pressure points, which occur when the macaw has to stand on perches of

Safe Tree Branches

✔ Apple	✔ Hawthorn
✔ Arbutus	✔ Larch
✔ Ash	✔ Magnolia
✔ Aspen	✔ Manzanita
✔ Beech	✔ Mulberry
✔ Birch	✔ Pear
✔ Cottonwood	✔ Pine
✔ Crab-apple	✔ Poplar
✔ Dogwood	✔ Redwood
✔ Elm	✔ Willow
✔ Fir	

uniform size. For larger macaws a diameter of 2 to 3 inches (5 cm–8 cm) is ideal, although some access to wider branches in addition helps to exercise the feet. New branches for perches should be supplied whenever the old branches have become dry and chewed beyond use. In addition, smaller branches can be routinely supplied at least once a week to provide occupational chewing material. Not all types of tree branches are suitable or safe for macaws and other parrots however.

Unsafe Tree Branches

The following types of tree branches from the *Prunus* genus of trees are not recommended because they contain cyanogenic glycosides, which can release cyanide if ingested:

✔ Apricot	✔ Prune
✔ Cherry	✔ Plum
✔ Peach	✔ Nectarine

DIET

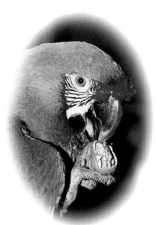

Providing a captive macaw with an appropriate diet is of great importance. Food fulfills not only your bird's nutritional requirements but its occupational needs as well. When a varied and well-prepared diet is offered, mealtime can prove to be the highlight of the bird's day. Macaws are more omnivorous than many other parrots and will readily try a new food that is offered. They have a well-developed sense of taste, and it cannot be denied that they derive great pleasure from eating their favorite foods.

General Considerations

Food should be prepared fresh every day. Be sure to purchase your bird's fruit and dry foods, such as seeds and nuts, from responsible suppliers who know how to properly handle and store their stock prior to sale. When feeding macaws remember that they are large, strong birds and any lightweight or unsecured food dishes that are offered to them are likely to be quickly tossed around and thrown to the floor. There are many different types of food dishes, and ways of securing them, so some experimentation will be needed to find the ones best suited to each bird.

A feeding shelf with a raised lip can prevent the food dish from sliding off but cannot stop a determined macaw from picking up the dish

A Hyacinthe macaw enjoys cracking a nut.

and tossing it off the shelf, as some are inclined to do. Many commercially available food and water dishes are secured by a metal holding frame and can be harder for the macaw to remove, ensuring that the food and water stay in place and are available to the bird throughout the day.

The quantity of food given to the bird daily must be monitored for two reasons. Hand-reared birds tend to be wasteful; when eating they throw much of their food out of the dish and onto the floor. Also, young birds can gain excessive weight if given unlimited amounts of their favorite foods. The exact amount of food that should be provided daily depends upon the species of macaw in question, the composition of the food offered, and the amount of daily activity/exercise the bird receives.

Generally, I find that even the larger macaw species live well on about a cup of mixed diet and a handful of assorted large nuts; smaller species require less.

To assess how much fat your macaw is carrying you need to feel the bird's chest and ribs: There should be a reasonable layer of fat covering the ribs so that they cannot be easily individually felt, although the fat must not make the chest feel rounded. If the bird's ribs can be easily felt and the central breastbone sticks out noticeably, the macaw is underweight and should receive increased food and a veterinary checkup to ensure that it is not ill or suffering from parasites. On the other hand, if the bird's chest is very rounded and firm, the bird is probably receiving too much food and is overweight, an indication that the food supply may have to be reduced.

A Balanced Diet

From personal experience, I feed macaws twice a day as I have found this the best way to ensure that they receive—and consume—a balanced diet. A balanced diet should be made up from a number of different food groups,

Sample Feeding Schedule

7:00 A.M.—Mixed fruit and vegetable salad: a mixture of regular fruit and vegetable items, with some variety of occasional/seasonal salad items.

2:00 P.M.—Pellet food with some dry seeds and nuts: Mainly pellet food (70 percent) with a mixture of seeds and nuts added (30 percent).

each of which will be discussed subsequently, but the key to success is ensuring that the macaw does eat most of the food items that are provided and does not selectively choose only its favorite foods. I follow a routine of feeding the birds twice a day, usually with the first feeding at 7:00 A.M., then a second feeding at 2:00 P.M. Using two separate feeding periods has two advantages. First, the provision of foods can be arranged to ensure that most items are consumed, and second, this regime allows for moist items (fresh fruits and vegetables) to be offered and consumed early in the day before the warmth of the midday and afternoon sun can lead to spoiling of these moist food items.

Fruits and Vegetables

A wide selection of fresh fruits and vegetables is generally available in most countries. You should look for variety, while ensuring balance in the diet. I would recommend a regular core of fruits and vegetables used in the morning salad as in the table on page 43, which should be periodically supplemented with a variety of other items to provide the pet macaw with variety in the diet.

Seeds and Nuts

Macaws tend to have a higher requirement for fat in their diet compared to many other parrot species. For many types of parrots, such as the Amazon parrots (genus *Amazona*) the use of dry seeds and oil-rich nuts has been almost entirely replaced by modern pellet diets now available to prevent the common problem of obesity in these species. With macaws however, I always include some dry seeds and nuts in the daily diet, unless the diet of a particular

Regular and Complementary Food Items for the Morning Salad Feeding

Regular Items for Daily Morning Feeding	Complementary Choices for Occasional/Seasonal Use
Apple	Strawberries
Pear	Peaches
Orange	Figs
Papaya	Banana
Grapes	Kiwi fruit
Tomato	Pomegranates
Green beans	Melon
Alfalfa	Plums
Lettuce	Apricots
Carrots	Baked Sweet Potato
Celery	Corn-on-the-Cob
Cucumber	Broccoli
Selection from complementary list	Onions
	Peppers
	Other safe seasonal fruits available locally

bird is being specifically limited due to a health problem. Preferred types of dry seeds include safflower, sunflower, and hemp. Preferred types of nuts include pine nuts, peanuts, and for larger species Brazil nuts, almonds, and macadamias. Care needs to be taken to ensure that the seeds and nuts are correctly stored and do not become spoiled by fungal or bacterial contamination before being fed to the pet bird.

Beans and Grains

A variety of beans and cereal grains can also be used in moderation as part of a balanced diet. The most commonly used types include mung beans, black-eyed beans, soy beans, barley, boiled maize, fresh corn, and lentils. Fresh soaked or boiled beans and cereals that have sprouted are of greater nutritional value than their dry state. All of the types of beans and cereals mentioned can be purchased easily and stored in dry condition prior to their use. The benefits of feeding sprouted beans and cereals are clear. They are an excellent source of protein, amino acids, and vitamins. The sprouting process does, however, need to be followed in great detail for hygiene; otherwise the sprouting process can becoming an ideal breeding ground for bacteria. It is recommended that an aviculturist with limited time and only a few birds should not attempt the sprouting of these beans, but instead provide these items to the bird in a boiled state. The protein, amino acids, and vitamins available from the sprouting process are today much more easily available from pellet food products that help to balance the captive diet.

Top left: A variety of fruits and vegetables should be included in the macaw's diet.
Middle left: Commercial pellet food that should be included in the macaw's diet.
Bottom left: Macaws love to have a variety of seeds and nuts.

Most commercial food dishes are designed to be firmly attached to the macaw's cage or perching.

Food and water dishes should be strong to prevent damage and be easy to clean.

Drinking water should be easily accessible to the macaw at all times.

TIP

Food Hazards

Avocados should *never* be included in the diet of a pet macaw. These are toxic to birds.

Pellet Foods

One of the major advances in bird nutrition and health care during the last decade of the 1990s was the establishment of several extremely good commercial brands of parrot pellet food. Pellet foods are a particularly good way of ensuring that the macaw receives a balanced nutritional content. Also, the extruded pellets are usually greatly enjoyed by pet macaws, which like to grind the pellets slowly while eating them. The main brands of commercial pellet food are now available with different levels of fat content. Higher-fat pellets are usually used for all macaw species, particularly for the Hyacinthine macaw. The names of several recommended manufacturers of pellet foods are given in Information, page 93. Pellet food products, with a higher fat level designed specifically for macaws, are highly recommended to constitute a large proportion of a pet macaw's diet.

Other Foods

Other food items can be occasionally used to supplement the macaw's diet. Pet macaws enjoy variety and new food items to explore. Some of the following might be tried as occasional food items.

Bread: Often many pet birds enjoy occasional slices of bread as a change from their usual diet. Whole wheat bread is a suitable occasional food item to provide a pet bird with a change from the ordinary.

Animal protein: Macaws in the wild will consume animal protein should a carcass be available. They have also been observed actually catching lizards and even small mammals occasionally to supplement their diet, particularly while rearing offspring. Captive macaws should receive a suitable amount of protein from their diet if a good-quality pellet food is included in their daily food mixture. Some owners still like to give their birds occasional pieces of meat, which are usually enjoyed by the birds. Any meat cooked in oil should be avoided, but lean, cooked meat and poultry make a welcome treat on an occasional basis. No raw meat should be given because of the risk of bacterial contamination.

Water and food dishes are best secured to the sides of the cage.

All water dishes—as well as food dishes—should be cleaned daily and replenished with fresh supplies.

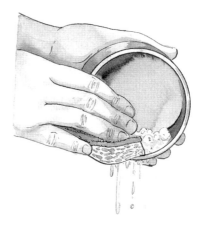

Vitamins and Minerals

With the advances that have taken place in aviculture over the last 20 years, a whole new range of specialized diets and supplements have become commercially available to the aviculturist. These diets are designed not only for use with birds in general, but also specifically for certain groups of birds such as the parrot family, which have more specialized requirements. Multivitamin and mineral powders can be added to the food supply, particularly the morning salad feeding, and prove extremely good at sticking to soft food items, such as fruit and vegetables, leading to an effective intake of the supplements by the bird.

A wide range of products is available. If the parrots are eating a well-balanced diet, they simply need a good, broad-spectrum multivitamin and mineral supplement specifically formulated for birds. If the bird is in poor health or is feeding only very selectively on certain food items, you should seek the advice of an avian veterinarian. In general, nutritional problems in captive macaws can be avoided if birds eat a varied diet including a reasonable amount of a good-quality pellet food.

Water Supply

Water is one of the most vital elements of life, even more important than food. Water is often taken for granted in many developed countries but it is worth greater attention when the welfare of birds is being considered. Water that is suitable for human consumption may not always be suitable for birds. In most developed countries the quality of drinking water is fairly good and captive birds adjust well. Sometimes, however, there can be problems whereby young chicks suffer from severe bacterial infections in the early stages of being reared, or new birds to a collection become sick. Investigation of these events frequently results in a problematic water supply. In many areas that are assumed to have good drinking water, such as Florida, aviculturists have experienced water quality problems that have adversely affected their birds, pseudomonas infection being one of the most common problems. Does your macaw appear to be weak for no obvious reason? Do the adult birds regularly appear to have enteritis? Are chicks lost in the nest box from what appear to be bacterial infections? You might consider the expense of having a microbiological examination of the birds' water supply a good, long-term investment.

HEALTH CARE

Macaws are among the hardiest and most long-lived of all the different types of birds that can be kept as a pet. Tame pet macaws develop their own distinct personalities and can form strong bonds with their owners; this kinship usually gives the owner a good understanding of the bird's behavior. If you notice a change in the bird's habits for which no obvious external explanation is apparent, look more closely—unusual behavior may well signal the beginning of a health problem.

Routine Health Care

Health care of your macaw does not begin when the bird becomes ill but is a daily concern that should be part of your day-to-day bird maintenance. Most of the steps in the health care routine can be regarded as common sense, but some of the more obvious considerations are listed below and deserve to be taken into account even before the actual purchase of a pet macaw.

Stress: Stress is an unseen but common killer of birds kept in captivity. Even captive-bred birds can suffer stress in the household environment. In most cases stress is not considered the direct cause of death, but it can be a strong

Healthy macaws should be bright eyed and alert, like this Severe macaw.

contributing factor in many health problems. The increased adrenaline and hormonal response that is triggered by stress can often weaken the physical condition of the bird, thereby reducing the effectiveness of its immune system. As a result, the bird is more susceptible to any number of possible infections that can take advantage of its weakened state.

Food supply: The food supply offered to a macaw must be freshly prepared each day and be of a balanced composition.

✔ All food items used in the diet, particularly fruit, should be of high quality.

✔ Food placed in an outside aviary must be protected from the elements and from all possible sources of contamination.

✔ Remember that native birds and rodents could drop feces onto the food if they have access to the food container and spread disease. In North America, opossums can carry a parasite in their feces that is fatal to pet birds.

✔ Care should be taken to exclude all possible disease vector animals from gaining access to the pet bird's food supply.

Water supply: Water is generally provided to the macaw in a dish secured to the side of the cage. It is essential that this container be cleaned and replenished daily with fresh water. Some pet macaws will not drink water that has been standing for a prolonged period. Additionally, an open water container can become contaminated by food items or feces dropped into it during the course of the day.

Health checkups: It is strongly advised that pet macaws receive a routine veterinary checkup; speak with your veterinarian to see if a regular checkup every six months or every twelve months is recommended. Such checkups can be of immense value in preventing illness and maintaining an accurate record of the macaw's general health. A standard biannual veterinary check up should include a blood sample analysis, fecal sampling, viral testing, and possibly vaccination for some diseases, such as Pacheco's virus (see page 54), if the veterinarian has concerns that such diseases are active in the regional area of the pet macaw.

Common Illnesses

Following are some of the most common illnesses that can occur in captive macaws. Preventive health care should hopefully make occurrences of ill health rare, but veterinary advice should be sought quickly if any signs of illness appear.

Vitamin Deficiencies

If macaws are fed a balanced diet, including a good-quality pellet food and dietary supplements, illness caused by vitamin deficiencies are unlikely. The most common deficiency that can occur is lack of vitamin A. Signs of vitamin A deficiency include swelling of the oral papillae, nasal discharge, watery eyes, and in severe cases, abscesses in the mouth. Vitamin A deficiency may contribute to the development of respiratory, digestive, and ocular diseases. Your veterinarian should be able to diagnose a vitamin deficiency problem and provide supplementation. This is usually provided by a short-term series of injections to correct the immediate effects of the deficiency, followed by long-term supplementation through the food supply to replace stores in the liver. Other possible vitamin deficiencies are less common and should be detectable by your veterinarian during routine health checkups.

Hypervitaminosis D

This condition is caused by an excess of vitamin D in the bird and causes a range of symptoms including kidney calcification, leading to death. This condition can be common in young macaws, which are very sensitive to receiving too much vitamin D in their diet through over-supplementation. This condition is best avoided by using a well-tested commercial food product for feeding young macaws and by not supplementing with additional sources of Vitamin D in the diet unless it is specifically under the direction of your veterinarian.

Ectoparasites (External Parasites)

Macaws can suffer from infestations of external parasites, such as ticks, lice, or mites. These parasites live on the surface of the skin and in the plumage, most commonly in warm humid areas such as under the wings. If external parasites are detected, then the cage environment needs to be thoroughly cleaned and any wooden perches changed.

Symptoms: Infested macaws are often restless and overpreen their feathers, often leading to dry and frayed plumage. Persistent scratching and bald areas of plumage are also symptoms, as is generally irritable mood behavior.

Treatment: The macaw should be treated with an appropriate safe insecticide product as recommended by your veterinarian.

Endoparasites (Internal Parasites)

A number of internal parasitic worms can infest captive macaws, the most common being roundworms (ascaridia), threadworms (capillaria), and tapeworms (cestoda). Infestation normally occurs by ingestion of the parasite egg stage, and thus is often associated with poor attention to cleanliness when birds are kept in outdoor cages. This infestation is not usually seen in pet macaws kept inside the home. Good standards of hygiene in any outdoor cage environment and careful preparation and protection of the food supply should prevent infestation from occurring.

Symptoms: Symptoms of internal parasite infestations are generalized signs of poor condition and weight loss. An infested bird may lose weight, have a ruffled feather appearance with slumped body posture, and have abnormal stool excretion.

Treatment: Infestation can be confirmed by screening a stool sample, so providing a stool specimen on the first visit to the veterinarian can facilitate a quick diagnosis and early treatment. The veterinarian can then prescribe the appropriate medication depending on the type of parasite detected.

Trichomoniasis

This is a protozoan condition. Usually this condition is not acute in adult birds but can become more serious in macaws where the physical condition is weakened by stress. Also, it can be a serious problem in young chicks, which become infected from food fed to them from an infected parent. Chicks are much more sensitive to protozoa and their condition can become acute if not diagnosed and treated.

Symptoms: Typical signs include loss of appetite and general discomfort of the bill. If the interior of the mouth can be viewed, the mucus can have a yellow appearance.

Treatment: Once an accurate diagnosis has been made your veterinarian will be able to prescribe an effective treatment.

Coccidiosis

Coccidia are single-celled parasites that live in the mucous membranes of the intestinal tract of the macaw.

Symptoms: Coccidia can cause severe inflammation of the mucous membrane, leading to intestinal bleeding, which can be seen as diarrhea, discolored stools, and weight loss.

Treatment: Once correctly diagnosed, your veterinarian can prescribe an effective treatment, usually a sulphur-based drug.

Bacterial Enteritis (Intestinal Inflammation)

This is one of the most common health problems seen in captive macaws, as possible causes of bacterial infections can be common in the

bird's living environment. Often a macaw can become more susceptible to a bacterial infection by pathogens in the living environment while under sudden periods of stress or when subject to a change in food or water supply.

Symptoms: General signs of poor health, such as slumped body posture and restlessness, often occur. Diarrhea is common in infected birds and often the vent feathers become dirty with stained excretion as a result. Increased drinking and loss of appetite can also be symptoms of bacterial enteritis.

Treatment: Prompt examination by a veterinarian is advised so that an appropriate antibiotic can be prescribed. This condition can be serious and life-threatening within a short period of time, so early detection and prompt veterinary assistance is important.

Salmonellosis

This disease is caused by the contamination of the macaw's food or water supply by salmonellae bacteria. This can occur when vectors, such as vermin, wild birds, or flies gain access to the food and introduce the salmonellae bacteria. If

Close attention to the hygiene of food and drinking water is essential for good health care.

salmonellosis is suspected, you should take care when handling the macaw or cleaning its cage as this disease can also be transmitted to humans.

Symptoms: Symptoms are very generalized. The bird simply appears to be in poor physical condition. Providing a stool sample for analysis on the first visit to the veterinarian can facilitate a quick diagnosis and early initiation of treatment.

Treatment: Once a correct diagnosis is made, an appropriate broad-spectrum antibiotic treatment can be prescribed by your veterinarian.

Aspergillosis

Aspergillosis is a fungal infection caused by molds. These are inhaled by the affected macaw leading to infection of the respiratory system. Fungal infections are usually associated with poor hygiene in the macaw's living environment, or with poor food storage and preparation. Thorough cleaning of the cage and careful attention to the freshness of food items should prevent the occurrence of this disease.

Symptoms: The most obvious sign is disturbed and labored breathing. Often a disturbance in the sound of the breathing, such as a rasping sound, can be heard that is suggestive of a blockage in the respiratory tract.

Treatment: Treatment is difficult once aspergillosis is in an advanced stage. Early detection of poor breathing by the bird is important, as is prompt veterinary assistance. An experienced avian veterinarian can control this condition in most cases. New advances in drug therapy are promising more effective treatment in the near future.

Respiratory Diseases (General)

Infection of the respiratory tract can have a multitude of causes, including bacterial, viral, or fungal diseases. Any infection of the respiratory tract can be serious regardless of cause; immediate veterinary advice should be sought if the bird has disturbed breathing.

Symptoms: Generalized symptoms can include sneezing, wet nostrils, discharge from nostrils, and labored and noisy breathing where the macaw sits in a slumped position and opens the beak to take breaths.

Treatment: Immediate veterinary advice should be sought to diagnose the nature of the respiratory infection. The bird should be kept warm and away from drafts until a diagnosis is made and appropriate treatment can be initiated by your veterinarian.

Ornithosis/Psittacosis (Chlamydiosis)

Ornithosis occurs commonly among psittacines (when referring to parrots the term psittacosis is frequently used for this disease) but is not a disease only of parrots. Many species of birds and mammals, and man, can be infected. Ornithosis can be transmitted from bird to bird or from bird to man, but transmission from man to bird or from man to man is not likely. The causative agent is *Chlamydia psittaci*, a bacterial organism, but unlike many common bacteria, *Chlamydia* can grow only inside a living cell. The organism, however, can remain dormant and infectious outside of the body. *Chlamydia* is shed in the feces and oral secretions of infected birds but can be shed intermittently.

TIP

Psittacosis

You should consider the possibility of psittacosis when dealing with a sick bird and be cautious of the general health significance.

✔ All sick birds should be isolated and excessive contact with people avoided.

✔ Young children, the old, or infirm are at a higher risk from psittacosis and in severe cases human symptoms can be seen as a severe flu-like illness characterized by high fever, headache, and respiratory illness. It can advance to a fatal pneumonia.

✔ Often, humans in good general health can also show only mild symptoms. If you experience any of these symptoms your doctor should be advised that you own or have had contact with birds.

Symptoms: When the bird is clinically ill, symptoms include diarrhea with bright yellow-green-colored feces, rapid weight loss, depression, nasal discharge, and red watery eyes.

Treatment: Accurate diagnosis can be difficult as the organism is shed intermittently. Once the veterinarian has confirmed the cause of illness, treatment with tetracycline or doxycycline may be effective in eliminating most infections; however, the birds do not develop immunity to the organism and are immediately susceptible to reinfection after cessation of treatment. When these birds become stressed or ill, the organism may attack the immune system and cause disease.

Viral Diseases

While less common than parasitic, bacterial, or fungal diseases, viral diseases can be quite devastating and are the primary reason for quarantine and judicious purchasing procedures. Viral diseases can be hard to diagnose and even harder to treat; the early involvement of a veterinarian is essential. For this reason the following virus diseases concentrate on recognizing symptoms, correct diagnosis, and discussion of treatment options that should be a function of your avian veterinarian.

Exotic Newcastle Disease

Viscerotropic Velogenic Newcastle Disease (VVND) is highly contagious and can affect virtually any avian species. The virus affects many organ systems and can cause signs of neurological disease as well as respiratory or digestive disease. The best prevention is to avoid the introduction of smuggled birds or birds imported without quarantine into a clean aviary. Captive-bred birds are very unlikely to be infected. U.S. law requires that any cases of this virus in North America be reported to the United States Department of Agriculture. All birds exposed to the virus will be seized and euthanized.

Polyoma Virus Infection

Polyoma virus infection can cause disease and mortality in macaw chicks especially in birds being hand-fed in a nursery facility or unweaned birds entering a pet shop. While adult birds are susceptible to infection, adults rarely become ill. Polyoma virus is widespread in aviculture and affects most parrot species. In susceptible chicks it can produce a fatal hepatitis. The incubation period is approximately 10 to 16 days. Clinical signs include depression, glassy eyes, hemorrhage

or bruising, and death. Virus is shed in the feces and oral secretions and transmission is direct or by contaminated objects such as hands or equipment. Polyoma virus is resistant to many common disinfectants including chlorhexadine. Chlorine bleach, quartinary ammonium disinfectants, or phenolic disinfectants may be required in case of an outbreak. In North America, a vaccine is available and is recommended for susceptible pet birds on veterinary advice.

Parrot Pox—Pox Virus Infection

The avian pox virus is a large DNA virus that is hardy and resistant to environmental factors so contaminated areas can be a source of infection. The virus is also transmitted by direct contact and by insect vectors such as mosquitoes. The incubation period is typically 7 to 14 days. Two forms are typically seen: the mild dry form and the severe wet form. In the dry form, dry, crusty lesions are found on the skin. When these scabs drop off the bird is immune. In the wet form, lesions may occur in the eyes, eyelids, mouth, respiratory system, and the skin of the feet, cere, beak, and nares. Clinical illness can continue for 2 to 6 weeks. Again, when lesions have healed the bird will be immune. This virus should be rare in captive-bred macaws, unless they have been exposed to an infected bird.

Pacheco's Parrot Disease

Pacheco's parrot disease (PPD) is a very contagious disease causing high mortality in parrots. PPD is caused by a herpes virus, which occurs naturally in South America. The incubation period is 5 to 14 days and death usually occurs with little or no visible sign of illness. Death is due to rapid and severe liver damage. Clinical signs include acute onset, depression, ruffled plumage, diarrhea, and bright yellow-green pigmentation of the stool, which is indicative of severe liver necrosis. Sinusitis, conjunctivitis, hemorrhagic diarrhea, conjunctivitis, convulsions, or tremors of the head, neck, wings, and legs may be seen. Although this virus is most commonly seen in wild-caught birds, captive parrots can sometimes act as carriers for the virus, leading to sporadic outbreaks. Drug therapy can be effective if administered early. A vaccine also exists in the United States, but some side effects have been reported.

Proventricular Dilatation Disease

Proventricular dilatation disease (PDD) is a serious disease of macaws. PDD is caused by a virus but at the time of writing the viral agent has not been identified. The virus causes inflammation of the nerves (ganglia), which innervate the crop, stomach, gizzard, and intestines. These organs lose their normal function or motility and dilate which results in maldigestion and wasting. Central nervous system signs are seen in some species and individuals. Clinical signs include weight loss, wasting, and passing whole seeds in the stool. Dilation of the proventriculus and ventriculus can be seen on X-rays. Confirmation can be made only by finding characteristic microscopic lesions in biopsy tissues (crop or proventriculus) or on necropsy, although biopsies can sometimes produce false negatives. Other diagnostic techniques are under investigation.

At this time no treatment is available, although a new treatment with the human drug Celebrex has shown some promise in preventing death. Mates of birds that die of PDD should be isolated pending future information on diagnosis and control. The disease occurs more frequently and spreads more rapidly in indoor facilities, so if possible, affected birds or flocks should be held in outdoor facilities where sunlight and natural ventilation help to destroy or dilute the virus.

Psittacine Beak and Feather Disease

Psittacine beak and feather disease (PBFD) is a viral disease affecting primarily old-world psittacines (species from Asia, Africa, and Australia). PBFD has been described in macaws but is uncommon in most neotropical psittacines; however, the effects of this virus can be devastating so symptoms should not be ignored if a macaw exhibits any signs associated with PBFD. The first detectable sign of PBFD is the appearance of necrotic, abnormally formed feathers. PBFD is characterized by the symmetric, progressive appearance of abnormal feathers during each successive molt. Abnormalities in feather growth can include retention of feather sheaths, hemorrhage within the pulp cavity, and fractures of the feather shaft. Short, clubbed feathers, stress lines within vanes, and circumferential constrictions may also occur in birds with this virus. Immediate veterinary advice should be sought if any of these abnormalities are seen in a pet macaw to check whether the bird may be suffering from this virus or from a behavioral problem.

Care of Ailing Birds

If the macaw is showing signs of poor health it can be assumed that illness has already taken hold and prompt attention and treatment will be required. For this reason, steps should be taken prior to encountering any health problems with the macaw to locate a veterinarian who is experienced in treating parrots and whose practice is within reasonable traveling distance.

Carrying box: The trip to the veterinarian's office will be a stressful event for the sick macaw. Therefore, every effort should be made to minimize its effects. A dark carrying box is best because any daylight entering the box will increase the macaw's awareness and anxiety will result. The box also needs to be well ventilated, but draft-free.

Warmth: Warmth is very important to an ailing bird. If the macaw is housed in an outside aviary, it should be caught and transferred indoors to a draft-free cage with a heat source maintaining a temperature of between 77 and 82°F (25–28°C).

Food and water: The macaw should have both food and water readily available within easy reaching distance of the perch it is sitting on. The placement of the food and water dishes within the cage may seem a trivial point, but in the case of a sick bird that does not feel compelled to eat or drink it is of great significance. If the dishes are too far away, the macaw might not make the small amount of effort needed to reach the food and water provided.

Hospital cages: Several types of commercial hospital cages are available, although the models that are suitable to house a large macaw can be very expensive for the average pet owner to purchase. A regular macaw cage situated in a draft-free room with a heat lamp placed over the top of the cage will serve the same purpose. The important feature of a good hospital cage is that it provide a warm, draft-free, and secure environment, which will greatly reduce the amount of stress the sick macaw is experiencing.

Behavioral Problems

Macaws kept as pets can develop adverse behavior, often referred to as *stereotype behavior*, which is a term used to describe habitual and exaggerated acts that the macaw may resort to in times of stress and boredom. When stereotype behavior is allowed to develop, it can become highly distressing to both the bird and its owner because it can manifest in a number of unpleasant ways. One of the most common is surely feather plucking, but other behavior can include repeated bouts of screeching and even self-mutilation. It is beyond the confines of this book to explore all of the possible behavioral problems that may be encountered and search for solutions, but a number of books concentrate upon this subject specifically, such as Barron's *Guide to*

Normal feather preening can sometimes lead to feather chewing if a bird is continually bored, too hot, too dry, or is generally uncomfortable.

a Well-behaved Parrot. Following is a brief discussion of the most common problems.

Screeching

Screeching can often occur in young pet macaws, most often when they go through their adolescence stage at between 18 and 36 months of age. The young bird will screech for the owner's attention if it is feeling ignored or neglected. At this age such screeching is not abnormal, but only represents the young bird trying to establish its will and gain the owner's attention. If repeated bouts of screeching are a problem in older birds, a closer examination of the bird's behavior is needed.

Feather Plucking

Feather plucking is perhaps the most widely seen behavioral problem in parrots. Often a young bird will begin to pull feathers from its wing or breast, but the plucking can turn into chewing and this can escalate to the point where a bird is completely missing all of the feathers that it can reach with its bill. This is a serious condition, which may in some cases be connected to a disease of dietary deficiency. If a young macaw is obviously beginning to exhibit this behavior, then an early visit to the veterinarian for a general checkup will help to show whether this is a pure behavioral problem, or if a skin infection, dietary deficiency, or disease may be a contributing factor.

Self-mutilation

Self-mutilation is a very harmful extension of the feather-plucking behavior. Sometimes a parrot will begin by chewing its feathers, but may then begin to chew at an area of its skin as well.

Commonly this will occur on the breast, leg, or area under the wing. If allowed to continue, the macaw will bite and chew the affected area resulting in bleeding, skin infection, and even wound infection. Such cases should receive immediate veterinary attention to treat the effects of the chewing behavior and to try and diagnose the reason why this behavior has begun.

Possible Causes

Possible triggers for the onset of stereotype behavior can include a change in the pet's environment—a change in owner or the presence of a new person or animal in the home—as well as a change in the bird's daily routine, such as a different feeding time or playtime. Hot weather can irritate the macaw if it is denied access to water for bathing or showering. Perhaps the most common cause is a sudden withdrawal or significant slackening of daily attention.

Preventing Behavioral Problems

✔ Spend more time playing with the macaw.
✔ Provide increased amounts of chewing wood.
✔ Keep the television and radio on longer.
✔ Provide a selection of macaw toys.
✔ Look for "toys" in the home, such as old wooden spoons and empty toilet paper rolls.
✔ Bring the bird out of the cage more often for mental stimulation, a change of scenery, and increased social contact.
✔ Try some new food items in the macaw's diet to provide mental and sensory stimulation.
✔ Provide increased access for bathing and/or showering.
✔ Have the macaw examined by an avian veterinarian to ensure that there is not a medical reason behind the behavioral problem.

When kept as pets, macaws usually develop highly individual but consistent behavior patterns. Excessive moodiness and other odd behavior can therefore be noticed fairly quickly and alert the owner that the bird may not be feeling completely well. Irritability and other moods can be brought on by external factors: For example, during periods of hot weather the macaw can become uncomfortable, particularly if it does not have access to bathing or showering. Despondency in a bird that cannot be reasonably explained, however, deserves

A sick macaw may have poor feathering, drooping wings, sleepy eyes, and will sit down upon its legs when perching.

serious attention, especially when accompanied by poor appetite and listlessness.

The physical posture of the macaw can also reveal possible signs of poor health. When a bird is healthy, it is alert and holds its head high watching all that is happening around it. Generally, a less firm than normal body posture with the head and wings drooped and the abdomen sagging over the feet can be a sign of illness. A sick bird will also be less alert and seem uncomfortable and unsure of its footing; often it can be observed shifting its weight from one foot to the other. Unexplained bulges in the bird's normally smooth feathering may conceal an abscess or cyst, which may result from an old injury that may have become infected. Remember that birds may feel self-conscious and threatened if observed from a close distance and may mask indications of poor health by appearing more alert then when they are relaxed and not under close observation. Therefore, when assessing a bird the initial observations should be made from a discreet distance. Only after the owner has gained an accurate idea of the bird's body posture when relaxed should the macaw be approached more

directly to look for other indications of poor health.

Eyes: The macaw's eyes can show signs of possible eye infections and give an indication of general poor health as well. The eyes of a healthy macaw are fully open and watchful. Illness can cause the macaw to be less observant and to partially close its eyes. Often, there can be swelling on the upper or lower eyelids and the eyes may appear watery; these are indications of an eye infection requiring veterinary attention.

Breath sounds: Breath sounds can also be a valuable guide to the macaw's state of health. Of course, when a macaw is inspected from a very close distance, its breathing will become rapid; this is not a bad sign but merely the bird's natural fight-or-flight response taking effect. By listening to the bird's breathing closely, several indications can often be gleaned: Although rapid, the breathing should not sound forced as this would suggest an obstruction within the respiratory tract. Likewise, rasping or other similar noises in the breathing can be a sign of loose patches of dead tissue that can result from aspergillosis or similar conditions.

The vent: If ill health is suspected in the macaw, you

should look at the vent to ensure that it has not become clogged with defecation and that the feathers surrounding it are not stained, which may indicate bacterial enteritis.

The chest: If the macaw is to be handled for a physical examination, the chest can then be gently felt for an indication of the bird's weight.

The mouth: The mouth can prove difficult to examine and any overzealous attempts to do so usually lead only to unacceptable levels of stress being inflicted on the bird, which may already be in a weakened state. Nevertheless, excessive amounts of saliva may be apparent even without direct examination of the interior of the bird's mouth. The macaw may appear uncomfortable and may repeatedly try to wipe its bill against the perches or other available objects.

A hospital cage. Heat and security are of prime importance to sick macaws.

Warning Signs

Contact your avian veterinarian for advice if any of the following symptoms of illness are noticed in the bird:
✔ Poor body posture.
✔ Disturbed breathing.
✔ Closed or "sleepy" eyes.
✔ Watery eyes.
✔ Nasal discharge.
✔ Change in normal behavior.
✔ Restlessness or aggressive behavior.
✔ Unexplained bulges in normally smooth plumage.
✔ Diarrhea and/or dirty vent feathers.

Preparation for the Veterinarian

When a serious health problem occurs, don't hesitate to seek the assistance of an avian veterinarian. To help the veterinarian quickly diagnose the cause of the health problem, be ready to answer the following questions:
✔ How long have you owned the macaw?
✔ Was the macaw wild caught or captive bred?
✔ Is the macaw housed alone or with other birds?
✔ When were the first signs of poor health noted?
✔ What symptoms did you notice?
✔ Have any other birds housed nearby shown similar problems?
✔ Has the macaw recently been subject to a change in its diet or water supply?
✔ Has the macaw recently been moved to a new cage or aviary?
✔ Has the macaw recently been introduced to a new mate or lost an established partner?
✔ Has the macaw experienced a previous illness? If so, what treatment did it receive?

If a serious ailment is suspected, providing a fecal sample on the first visit to the veterinarian can be very helpful; the correct diagnosis can thus be obtained rapidly and treatment can be initiated.

BREEDING MACAWS

Most species of macaws will breed readily in captivity providing their needs for mate selection, seclusion and security, diet, and appropriate nest sites are met. Captive breeding is essential for the continued presence of macaw species in the pet market. With the import of wild parrots now strictly regulated in most western countries, almost all macaws that will be available to the pet owner will have been domestically bred.

Sexing Macaws

Throughout the history of aviculture macaws have been bred in captivity. Some pairs in early aviculture have been described as being quiet prolific once successful breeding had been initiated. However, if one considers the large numbers of macaws that have been available to aviculture, the level of historical breeding success prior to the 1970s was poor. Probably the main reason is that in the past decades, macaw owners had to guess at sexing their birds based on subtle physiological differences and observations of the bird's behavior. The advent of surgical sexing techniques—using the endoscope to view the sex organs of a bird—has seen a dramatic increase in successful cap-

A young hand-reared Hahn's macaw chick still has an immature eye color.

tive breeding of macaws. Even more recently, techniques of sexing birds by the examination of chromosomes or DNA material have made accurate sexing even easier as macaws can now be sexed by a small blood or feather sample, without the need for a surgical operation.

Sexing Macaws by Physical Characteristics

Physical differences between the male and female gender of macaws do exist, although the extent of the differences are subtle and subject to interpretation. Often the individual differences in terms of size, weight, and physiology within a group of specimens can be more noticeable than the differences between the sexes.

In general, the adult male of a macaw species will have a slightly larger head than the female.

Its bill will also be slightly more prominent, particularly at the base, where along with the cere it can be noticeably wider than that of a female. However, given the wide variability between individual specimens, such physical indications are very much open to interpretation and are not always reliable. Therefore, such subjective differences should never be completely relied upon, especially when other more accurate sexing techniques are available today.

Sexing Macaws by Behavioral Characteristics

Observing the interactions of a group of macaws during social courtship and pair-bonding behavior is very interesting, but is not a completely reliable way to sex macaws. Mistakes can be made if the gender ratio within the social group is not balanced. If a suitable potential mate of the opposite gender is not available, often two birds of the same gender can form a "dominant/recessive" relationship and behave much like a true pair, even to the extent of going through courtship and mating gestures. For this reason, macaws should always be accurately sexed, either surgically or by DNA analysis, and then be marked to prevent confusion. After marking, the birds' behavior can then be studied to select bonded pairs without the risk of mistakenly pairing up two birds of the same sex.

Endoscopic Sexing of Macaws

Endoscopy (sometimes also called laparoscopy) is a surgical examination of the sex organs performed through an endoscope. This instrument consists of a thin elongated probe that is about 6 inches (15 cm) long and 1¼ inches (3 mm) in diameter; a fiber optic cable runs through the center of this tube and transmits light from an attached source to facilitate viewing. An experienced veterinarian using this equipment will insert the probe into the macaw's left abdominal air sac and view the bird's sex organs through an eye piece situated at the other end of the probe. This allows the correct gender of the bird to be confirmed by direct observation. Some individual birds can be harder to sex by this method than others. This is most commonly due to obesity; an excess of fatty tissue can obstruct the view of the sex organs.

The main drawback with endoscopy is the potential risk associated with any form of surgical procedure on a bird, however simple the procedure might be. Care should be taken to prevent undue stress to the bird prior to and after the operation, especially during catching and transporting of the macaw to the place where the surgery is to be performed. It is normal practice not to feed the macaw on the day of the operation so the digestive tract will be empty, to minimize any complications.

DNA and Chromosomal Sexing of Macaws

Alternatives to the surgical procedure are techniques now available that allow for the sex of a bird to be determined by laboratory examination of a blood or feather sample from the bird. A number of companies now offer this service; advertisements can be found in the pages of reputable pet bird magazines. The exact type of sample to be collected from the macaw depends upon the specific technique being used. Some research companies examine the bird's DNA, while other companies examine live chromosomes. The type of sample usually requested is a drop of blood, which can be obtained by clipping a toenail or pulling out a blood feather. You should contact companies that advertise in the pages of respected pet bird magazines and review the information provided by the company on how samples will need to be collected and transported.

Record Keeping

Keeping good records is a priority for all pet owners and bird breeders. As the importation of wild macaws has all but stopped in most Western countries, keeping proper records of parentage will become ever more important if birds currently available as breeding stock will form the basis of long-term, sustainable populations. It has already become apparent in recent decades that the intensive use of artificial rearing techniques to increase breeding success has resulted in a large proportion of the young birds reared in captivity being the offspring of a small percentage of the available genetic material.

Additionally, keeping accurate records can be of direct help to you when you need to check on routine bird husbandry matters such as worming, previous illnesses and treatments, feather clipping, egg-laying seasonality, changes in the bird's diet, accommodation of partners, and so on. The record card should also contain notes about anything unusual that may be observed in the bird's behavior, even slight signs such as poor appetite, listlessness, or poor body posture. As previously discussed, these could be the first visible signs of illness; having an accurate, dated record of them can prove valuable to the veterinarian in making a diagnosis at a later date.

CHECKLIST

Information That Should Be Recorded by the Macaw Owner
✔ Courtship behavior.
✔ Date of egg laying.
✔ Change of cage or cage partner.
✔ Changes in pairing of breeding birds.
✔ Parentage of chicks.
✔ Changes in diet or water supply.
✔ Any signs of poor health.
✔ Routine medical care.
✔ Treatments prescribed by the veterinarian.
✔ Feather clipping.
✔ Cleaning of nest box.

Pair Bonding

The advent of accurate sexing techniques for monomorphic species of birds, such as macaws, has over the past decades helped revolutionize captive breeding. It is by no means enough, however, to merely house together a male and female of the same species for them to breed. Macaws are highly intelligent and sociable; when given the chance they spend much time indulging in social interaction with their peers. Therefore, it is not surprising that the strong bonds developed by breeding pairs are not the result of random pairings, but rather of individual selection of partners. Macaws are highly individual in their behavior; they can exhibit a strong attraction as clearly as a strong dislike for another individual. The random pairing of two macaws of different gender does not

Sexing macaws, such as these Green-winged macaws, by appearance can be misleading and inaccurate.

guarantee that breeding will follow. Incompatible pairings can also prove distressing for one or both of the macaws involved; such a situation can potentially lead to stress and even aggression if the incompatibility is not noticed and managed.

To avoid mistakes in pairing, macaws should be given every chance to select their own future mates. Prior to introducing macaws into a social aviary, each bird should be correctly sexed and identified with a clear visual marking system. Soon after the birds have been introduced, close observation should be undertaken to ensure that no immediate aggressive situations are allowed to develop. To reduce the risks of aggression in social pairing flight, macaws are usually introduced during the nonbreeding season. During the main breeding season the birds will have increased sexual excitement, and hormone levels of male birds will be raging, making them increasingly competitive and potentially aggressive. Once birds have been introduced in the nonbreeding season and no immediate aggression has been observed, then more subtle study can begin in

order to observe how the birds are interacting with each other. Once obvious pairs have been formed then they should be separated from the social aviary and placed into a breeding aviary.

Maintenance of Breeding Aviaries

The subject of accommodation has already been discussed in the chapter on Housing (page 29), but it is worth looking more closely at some aspects of aviary preparation and daily management that are relevant during the breeding season.

When a pair of macaws is incubating a clutch of eggs or a brood of chicks, its overwhelming need is for seclusion and a sense of security. It is common practice to use vision breaks between aviaries during the breeding season to reduce direct sight between breeding pairs; otherwise, males from adjoining aviaries can become aggressive at the sight of each other and this can lead to tension building up between the pair itself.

Routine maintenance, feeding, and cleaning of the aviary should be carried out as quickly as possible to cause minimal disturbance. However, good levels of hygiene should still be maintained and cleaning should still be a daily routine to prevent increased attention from vermin from become a problem. Macaws will require a ready supply of food while they are rearing offspring. The amount of food provided should be increased to meet their food consumption requirements, but be sure to remove all unwanted leftover food.

Nest Boxes

Many different nest box designs have been used successfully to breed macaws in captivity. The most common is the "grandfather clock" type of nest box, which is usually constructed to be about three times the macaw's own body length in height and one body length in width and depth. Other kinds of nest box include the horizontal version of the grandfather clock design, a nest constructed from a barrel, and a whole assortment of different versions of these shapes, the most common of which are illustrated on page 66.

Requirements

To determine which type of nest box may best encourage the macaws' breeding attempts, you need to consider what factors are important to the birds.

✔ Seclusion and a sense of security within the nest box are of paramount importance; therefore, the box should be of sturdy construction.

✔ The amount of daylight that penetrates to the interior of the nest also affects the birds' sense of security. Macaws like dark, secluded nest sites. Nest boxes for macaws should be placed in the sheltered and shady area of the aviary for this reason.

✔ A large nest box with a small entrance hole should ensure that once inside the female can prepare her nest, in a position where sunlight

Behavioral interaction between macaws can sometimes provide a clue to sexual gender. But this method is not foolproof.

cannot penetrate. The size of the entrance hole should be just large enough for the birds to pass through; a small entrance hole is more easily defendable and has less light penetration, thus increasing the feeling of security for the inhabitants.

✔ If a vertical style of nest box is used, a ladder consisting of wooden blocks secured to the interior of the front panel will be necessary to allow the adults, and later the fledgling chicks, to climb easily to the entrance hole of the nest. Additionally, the interior walls of the nest box can have several blocks of chewing wood secured to them in a random pattern that, without restricting the movements of the macaws within the box, will provide occupational chewing material for the adult birds while inside of the nest.

✔ The nesting medium used inside the nest box should be fresh, large-sized wood shavings that have been strained to remove unnecessary dust before use. The type of wood used to

produce the shavings and chewing wood inside of a nest box should be as recommended as safe in the chapter on Housing (page 29).

✔ The floor of the nest box should have between 4 and 8 inches (10 cm–20 cm) of fresh wood shavings.

The Site

Once the nest box is prepared, the next decision concerns site selection: Where's the best spot to place the box within the aviary? As already mentioned, macaws prefer secluded, shaded areas for nest sites where protection from the elements and direct sunlight are available. Wherever possible, the entrance hole to the box should be well above the head height of the owner; remember that macaws derive a greater feeling of security from such a higher placement of the box. From personal experience, I generally prefer to place nest boxes on the side wall of the aviary if the aviary is on public display or in a heavily trafficked area. Macaws will feel threatened if, upon emerging from the entrance hole of the box, they must look

straight into the faces of those standing outside the aviary looking in.

Inspection Flap

For easy maintenance, the nest box should include an inspection flap that allows the interior of the box to be examined with as little disturbance as possible. Nest box inspections while the macaws are breeding should be kept to a minimum, especially in the case of macaws that are not yet breeding consistently. When the macaws are permitted to rear their own offspring, they should be allowed to incubate their eggs without disturbance from nest inspections until the time when the eggs are due to hatch, unless, of course, the adult bird's behavior gives cause for concern. A brief inspection at the time when the eggs are due to hatch is appropriate to ensure that the eggs are indeed fertile and alive; if not, the eggs can be removed to save the female from extended incubation of eggs that are infertile or have died.

Cleaning

The nest box should be cleaned once the chicks have fledged. Often pairs of macaws, which have settled into consistent breeding behavior, can rear more than one brood of chicks each year. The owner should therefore try to ensure that the nest box is clean and provided with fresh shavings before the female begins to lay a new clutch of eggs. At the end of the breeding season the nest box should be removed and fully serviced, thoroughly cleaned, and any necessary repair work attended to. Care should always be taken to

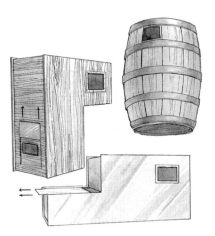

Various types of nest boxes for macaws to breed in are available.

ensure that the wood used in the box construction, for wood shavings, and for blocks of chewing wood is from a safe untreated source (not treated with any harmful chemicals such as preservatives). Throughout the breeding season, the interior of the nest box and the wood shavings in particular should be checked periodically to ensure that no parasites (mites or ticks) are present. If parasites are detected, the interior of the nest box should be treated with a safe antiparasite powder, as recommended by your veterinarian.

Egg Laying

Most species of macaws lay clutches of between two and five eggs. Details of species variation are described in the individual species descriptions at the end of this book (page 73). Nearly always, eggs are laid in the early part of the day. In larger species, the eggs are laid in a series with approximately 48 hours between each egg. In some of the smaller macaw species the time interval between each egg can be longer, up to 72 hours.

Incubation usually starts soon after the first egg has been laid; this means that the resulting chicks will hatch at time intervals of between two to three days between each, depending upon the species. This accounts for the fact that as a brood of chicks is reared, there is almost always a noticeable size difference between each chick. The first chick, being the largest, is always the most likely to survive under normal circumstances, but as long as enough food is available, the parents will ensure that the entire brood receives enough food to be reared through to independence. The incubation period for most species of macaw is between 26 and 28 days. Variation between species is described in the individual species descriptions at the end of this book (see page 73).

Artificial Incubation

If for some reason a clutch of eggs needs to be removed from the parent birds, artificial incubation can be accomplished easily with the correct equipment and preparation. To succeed in incubating macaw eggs by artificial means, by those who have limited experience, some factors need to be understood.

Temperature

Eggs require an extremely constant temperature to develop and hatch successfully. Most macaw breeders agree that the ideal temperature for incubating macaw eggs is 99.3°F (37.4°C), although temperatures that are one- or two-tenths higher or lower should prove successful if maintained at a constant level throughout incubation.

Weight Loss

An egg will lose weight during the incubation process as water is lost through evaporation and is replaced by a growing air sac, normally situated inside of the base the egg. The oxygen inside the air sac will be used during the hatching process by the developing chick to gain the strength necessary to break through the egg's shell.

The correct rate of water loss is essential if the chick is to hatch in good health. When the egg loses too much water too quickly, the air sac will grow larger than normal, which will restrict the space for the developing chick. This in turn can lead to failure in hatching or

result in small weak chicks that usually have severe problems in assimilating calcium and often die. On the other hand, if the egg does not lose enough water, the reverse is true. The air sac may not grow sufficiently to hold enough oxygen for the chick to hatch. Also, the chick will have to absorb the excess albumen before hatching.

Humidity is the factor that directly affects the rate at which water is lost from the egg. Too high a level will slow the rate at which water is lost from the egg because the air is already saturated with moisture, whereas a drier atmosphere will lead to a greater rate of water loss.

To develop appropriately, the egg should lose between 13 percent to 18 percent of its initial weight between the time that it is laid until the chick pips by breaking through into the air sac. The most significant period for the pattern of weight loss to be established is during the first 15 days of the incubation period. The weight loss of the egg should be measured at regular time intervals. Its progress can be assessed by preparing a weight loss graph or by using the following simple equation.

$$\frac{\text{Fresh laid egg weight} (\times) \text{ desired percentage loss}}{\text{Number of days to pip}}$$

A two-day-old Blue and Gold macaw chick is being hand-reared.

The number of days until pip is normally two days less than the full incubation period. The result of this equation is the daily amount of weight that should be lost by the egg if it is to hatch successfully.

Egg Turning

While she incubates her eggs, the macaw hen will rotate and move them randomly. Egg turning is important for several reasons, the most important of which are that it aids water loss, ensures that the yolk does not stick to one particular piece of shell, and allows the developing veins to spread more easily in the albumen. Artificial incubation must simulate the turning actions of the hen. Most commercially manufactured incubators are equipped with automatic turning devices, such as tilting trays or rollers. Some incubator turning devices primarily developed for poultry may create too much vibration for parrot eggs so check with the manufacturer before purchasing one. It is best to turn the eggs at least seven (or more) times each day, with a regular time interval (two hours) between each turn. When being turned, the egg should be rotated at least 180 degrees, always in alternating directions.

Candling: As an egg develops through the incubation period its stage of development can be visually monitored by a technique called "candling." This is done by shining a directed light source into the egg to illuminate its interior. Although growth rates can vary, there are definite signs that become visible at certain stages of the egg's development. By the fifth day of incubation there should be clear evidence of fertility—a small red dot with a sharp red circle surrounding it. Growth of the embryo can be clearly seen by the tenth day, as well as veins extending down one side of the egg's interior. At about 24 days the available space within the egg, excluding the air sac, should be filled by the embryo's development and a shadow of the chick's bill pushing into the membrane of the air sac should be visible if the chick has not already broken through and achieved internal pip.

Hatching

After the chick has broken through into the air sac it is time to move the egg from the main incubator into the hatching incubator. The hatching incubator has three significant differences.

1. First, the egg is no longer turned as it has already started the hatching process.

2. Second, once the chick begins the hatching process and pips through the exterior shell of the egg, the rate of water evaporation will rapidly increase, so the hatching incubator is maintained at as high a level of humidity as possible. This is to prevent the chick from drying out before completing its emergence from the shell.

3. Third, toward the end of its incubation process, the chick is almost fully formed and begins to generate its own body heat as it starts to struggle to hatch. For this reason, hatching incubators are maintained at a lower temperature, about 1° lower than normal incubation temperature; otherwise, the extra heat generated by the chick's exertions, together with the higher level of humidity, could soon tire the chick, making it difficult to complete the hatching process.

After hatching, the chick should be allowed to dry in the hatching incubator for at least six hours before being removed and taken to a brooder that has been prepared in advance, ready to begin the hand-rearing process.

Hand-rearing Macaws

The preparation for hand-rearing a macaw should take place well in advance of the estimated date of hatching. When newly hatched, although most aspects of the chick's biology are fully functional, a macaw chick is unable to control its body temperature and is extremely weak. The chick will not be able to support itself in an upright body posture and will not be able to feed by itself. Therefore, matters such as appropriate housing, temperature control, diet, feeding schedule, and hygiene must be considered in advance by the owner. Immediately upon leaving the hatching incubator, the young macaw chick will need to have all of its requirements met by the attention of the person hand-rearing it; everything should be prepared and ready at this time.

A Blue and Gold macaw chick is hand-fed with a syringe.

Housing Young Chicks

Because the newly hatched macaw chick is unable to properly control either its movements or its body temperature, it will need to be housed inside a brooder where both of these functions can be controlled. There are many types of commercially manufactured brooders available, which should all prove suitable if the manufacturer's instructions are followed.

✔ The brooder should be large enough to accommodate the young macaw as it grows, as well as a container for it to sit in during the first weeks of the rearing period.

✔ The interior of the brooder should be easy to maintain because strict cleaning and disinfecting routines will be required.

✔ The brooder should have been constructed to ensure that there are no exposed areas of electrical wires or other potentially dangerous items that are accessible to the macaw chick.

✔ The brooder should have been set up and left running for several days prior to the expected hatching date of the macaw chick to ensure the stability of the temperature maintained within the brooder.

✔ The macaw chick should be placed inside a small, easy-to-clean container. The bottom of the container should be covered with absorbent paper toweling, which should be changed at every feeding period. The removed paper toweling should be examined to ensure that the chick is excreting normally. Additional absorbent paper toweling can be used to pad the sides of the container to allow the chick to comfortably lean against the side to help support an upright body posture. The ability to maintain an upright body posture is particularly important after a chick has been fed because the weight of the food inside its crop can unbalance the young chick.

✔ The container that the macaw chick is placed in, and all interior surfaces of the brooder, should be cleaned daily with a safe disinfectant.

Temperature

The brooder must be kept at an appropriate temperature for the young macaw chick to grow and thrive. As a general guide, the initial brooder temperature should be about 97°F (36°C) for the first five days after hatching. From the sixth day on the temperature should be decreased by about half a degree each day until the temperature in the brooder nears room temperature as the chick becomes feathered and strong enough to better regulate its own body temperature. Every chick is individual, however, and will grow and develop at its own rate of progress. Because of this, the temperature level must be adjusted to suit the individual requirements of the chick. At the correct temperature, the young chick will have a healthy light pink coloration and sleep comfortably, but will also be lively and active when being fed. If the temperature of the brooder is too cold, then the chick will have a paler complexion, will lose interest in feeding, become inactive, and may even shiver. If, on the other hand, the brooder temperature is too hot, the chick will have a reddish skin coloration, will be unsettled and overactive, may regurgitate its food, and will not be able to sleep comfortably.

Diet

A great variety of homemade diets have been used to hand-rear macaws in captivity during the last three decades; in recent years, however, the advent of advanced, commercially produced hand-rearing diets have replaced the need for macaw owners to formulate their own. I have hand-reared many macaw chicks on the commercial diets "Exact," manufactured by Kaytee Products, Inc., and also the 12 percent fat formula manufactured by Pretty Bird International, Inc. Advertisements for these formulas, as well as for other brands, can be found in the pages of pet bird magazines or at any large pet retail company specializing in pet birds. Each formula comes with instructions from the manufacturer about the correct preparation of the food, and these instructions should be followed without variation. The food should be prepared and fed to the chick at a temperature of 104°F (40°C). The food formula should be freshly prepared at each feeding period.

Feeding Schedule

When first removed from the hatching incubator and placed inside the brooder, the chick should not be fed for several hours. This is to allow the newly hatched chick to dry and regain its strength after hatching. The delay also helps ensure that the majority of any remaining yolk inside the chick's abdomen has had the opportunity to be absorbed before oral feeding begins. In the case of a chick that has had a difficult hatching process and has become dehydrated, an exception can be made and the chick given a small amount of hydration fluids as soon as it has settled into the brooder temperature and seems comfortable. Details of a feeding schedule are normally provided with the food product by the manufacturer. I generally feed young macaws on a daily basis at regular time periods between 6:00 A.M. and midnight.

The chick can be fed either with a shaped spoon or by a syringe. It should be fed slowly and care should be taken not to overfill the crop, particularly during the first week; look out for a stretched and shiny appearance of the crop skin that will indicate that it has been overfilled. It is normal to begin feeding the chick early in the morning at around 6:00 A.M., and then to feed it repeatedly throughout the day each time the crop is nearly empty. As the chick grows the crop capacity will expand to hold a larger quantity of food and the frequency of feeding will lessen. Soon the chick will require only six feeds per day, then four feeds, up until the beginning of weaning when a fully feathered macaw will be receiving only two feeds of hand-rearing formula per day as it starts to experiment feeding itself.

Weaning Macaws

As the macaw starts to eat food by itself, it begins the weaning process. During this time some amount of weight loss occurs. The weight and physical condition of the bird need to be closely monitored to ensure that the weight loss is not so dramatic as to affect the health of the bird. The macaw should not lose more than 10 percent of its highest weight recorded prior to the beginning of weaning. Macaws wean at their own rate. Weaning is a learning process for the bird that cannot be hurried or carried out faster than the bird is comfortable with.

A macaw in the company of brood mates, or other birds of similar species and age, will learn to wean faster as it watches its companions also experimenting with food. Young macaws at this age are becoming quite conscious of their surroundings and are starting to look for mental stimulation from the environment that surrounds them.

Most authorities today recognize 17 living species of macaws (although one species may in reality be extinct), which have been divided into four separate generic groupings. Most macaw species considered suitable as pets fall within the first and largest genus of Ara.

Genus Ara

The genus of *Ara* contains 12 living species of macaw, with at least two known species that have long since become extinct—the St. Croix macaw *(Ara autocthones)* and the Cuban macaw *(Ara tricolor)*. The 12 species vary greatly in size and color, although all share a similar shape. *Ara* macaws have long, graduated tail feathers and large broad heads with bills that are ample and pronounced. The most noticeable taxonomic feature of these birds is the area of bare skin on both sides of the face. The facial patches can be either completely bare or to some degree covered by rows of small facial feathers, varying between species. All species are monomorphic, meaning that there are no obvious differences between the sexes.

A variety of different macaw species can be found at bird parks and other sanctuaries.

Green-winged Macaw

Ara chloroptera
CITES Appendix II

Description: Length 36 inches (90 cm). This is the largest species within the genus of *Ara*. Plumage coloration covering the head, throat, breast, stomach, thighs, upper back, and lesser wing coverts is a rich, dark red. Much of the central band of the wing is green, including the inner secondaries, tertials, and scapulars, which provide the bird its common name. The remainder of the wing feathers—the primaries, secondaries, and greater wing coverts—are a dark blue color with lighter blue also covering the lower back, rump, upper and undertail coverts, and the tips of the red tail feathers. The facial area is bare with the exception of several rows of very small feathers, giving the impression of thin red lines painted on the bare pale skin. The upper mandible is light gray with darker edging at the lower base; the lower mandible is black. Legs are gray. The iris is pale yellow.

Distribution: The Green-winged macaw has a wide range across much of northern South

America, including eastern Panama, northwestern Colombia east of the Andes, Venezuela, the Guianas, northern Brazil, northern and eastern Bolivia, and eastern Paraguay.

Habitat and status: The Green-winged macaw can be encountered in a variety of habitats across its range, but is perhaps most at home in primary humid lowland forests up to 3,300 feet (1,000 m) in altitude. This species, although extremely widespread, is noted for being less gregarious than other species, and therefore is rarely seen in large flocks. Yet, it is possibly the most widely distributed and numerous of the wild macaws.

Personality: The Green-winged macaw is well established in captivity with captive breeding now common. It is known to have appeared in aviculture as far back as the seventeenth century, although regular and consistent breeding in captivity was not achieved until the 1980s. This is not the easiest of the larger macaws to breed and therefore its price has remained slightly higher than for the more prolific species, such as the Blue and Gold macaw (Ara ararauna). However, the pet potential of the Green-winged macaw is very strong, if the owner can suitably accommodate such a large macaw. The Green-winged macaw is somewhat quieter and more affectionate than many other macaw species. It is one of the "gentle giants" among the Ara genus of macaws. The slightly larger size also gives this species a much more impressive appearance, particularly in relation to the head and bill, which are extremely pronounced and imposing. Hand-reared Green-winged macaws can prove to be among the best pets, although the owner should be aware of the strength of the bird's bill and its destructive potential if given freedom within the household environment.

Breeding: When compared to other species, wild-caught Green-winged macaws may take longer to settle in captivity and require more time to select a mate and form a strong pair bond. Today, however, most Green-winged macaws that are available have been domestically bred, so breeding has become more consistent. The normal clutch size is two to three eggs; incubation takes 26 days and begins soon after the first egg has been laid. After hatching, a parent-reared chick will be ready to fledge after 14 weeks of age; hand-reared chicks by comparison may take longer to wean and become independent.

Scarlet Macaw

Ara macao
CITES Appendix I

Description: Length 33 inches (85 cm). In general appearance the Scarlet macaw is superficially similar to the Green-winged macaw, but is smaller with brighter coloration and can be distinguished by the broad yellow band across the wing over the greater and medium wing coverts. The main body plumage of the Scarlet macaw is a noticeably lighter shade of red than for the previous species. This extends over most of the body, with the exceptions of the lower back, rump, and upper and undertail coverts, which are light blue. A darker blue covers most of the flight feathers as well as the tips of the yellow wing coverts and red tail feathers. The face is bare except for a few small feathers showing on the pale skin. The bill is creamy gray on the upper mandible but darkens to black at the base; the lower mandible is black. The legs are gray and the iris is brown.

Distribution: Although no recognized subspecies are recorded for the Scarlet macaw, at least two distinct populations are recognized that demonstrate a visual difference in the extent of the yellow band across the wing. The populations from Central America, found from the state of Oaxaca in Mexico down to southern Panama, have a broad yellow band across the wing. The extent of the yellow band across the wing is much reduced in the main South American population; ranging from east of the Andes, from Colombia to Bolivia, and eastward across Brazil to Guiana and the island of Trinidad.

Habitat and status: The Scarlet macaw has an extensive range, but is most frequently encountered in humid primary forests, or more open secondary forests and woodlands below 3,300 feet (1,000 m) in altitude. Although widely distributed, the Scarlet macaw is becoming increasingly rare across much of its range, particularly in Central America.

Personality: The Scarlet macaw has been common in captivity for more than a century and has proved very willing to breed in aviculture. Therefore, even though the Scarlet macaw is listed in Appendix 1 of CITES, enough captive-bred specimens have long been available to ensure its presence in North American aviaries to allow young hand-reared birds to be readily available as pets, despite the endangered status of this species in the wild. Young Scarlet macaws can make good pets but require much time and attention from the owner if they are to remain tame as they mature. The personality of young Scarlet macaws can be much more boisterous and aggressive than other macaw species commonly kept as pets.

Breeding: The Scarlet macaw has for many years proved very willing to breed consistently in captivity. Today, nearly all of the birds available are captive bred. The clutch size is usually between two to four eggs; incubation period is 26 days beginning soon after the first egg is laid. After hatching, when parent-reared, Scarlet macaws will be ready to fledge after about 11 weeks of age. Hand-reared chicks will take longer to become independent.

Blue and Gold Macaw
(also called Blue and Yellow Macaw)
(Ara ararauna)
CITES Appendix II

Description: Length 34 inches (86 cm). Most of the upper body, from the crown of the head reaching down the back and over upper-wings and tail, is blue. The undertail coverts are also blue. The front of the crown is greenish blue and the forehead green. The undersides of the body are nearly all a rich yellow; this color covers the entire breast, stomach, and thighs, and reaches up the sides of the face to the bare skin around the eye. The only other main coloration is a black patch that reaches around the underside of the bird's throat. The bare skin on the side of the face has several fine lines of small black feathers; the bill is also completely black. The legs are dark gray and the iris is yellow.

Distribution: The Blue and Gold macaw is widely distributed over northern South America, including Colombia, southern Venezuela, Brazil, the Guianas, Trinidad, northern Bolivia, northern Peru, eastern Panama, and Ecuador.

Habitat and status: The Blue and Gold macaw is a bird of lowland forests, rarely found above 1,650 feet (500 m) in altitude. The preferred habitat is humid primary forest, although it can be found less frequently in secondary forest. This is perhaps the most numerous and least threatened of the larger wild living macaws.

Green-winged macaw (Ara chloroptera).

Scarlet macaw (Ara macao).

Personality: The Blue and Gold macaw is by far the most widely seen, and most frequently kept of the larger pet macaw species. The Blue and Gold macaw has been known in aviculture since the eighteenth century with the first known captive breeding being recorded as long ago as 1818. Young Blue and Gold macaws have a generally good personality and when handled regularly make excellent pet birds. Little more needs to be said considering how widely and successfully the Blue and Gold macaw is kept as a pet bird.

Breeding: The Blue and Gold macaw been very consistently in captivity for many years; it was perhaps the first of the larger macaws to become firmly established into a strong, self-sustaining captive population. The clutch size is usually between two and four eggs; incubation period is 26 days, beginning soon after the first egg is laid. The Blue and Gold macaw is noted for its willingness in aviculture to produce up to three (or even four) clutches of eggs in the same year if the eggs or chicks are removed from the parent's nest box. After hatching, parent-reared, young chicks will fledge by the age of 14 weeks; hand-reared chicks may take longer to become independent.

Blue-throated Macaw
(also called Caninde Macaw)
Ara glaucogularis
CITES Appendix I

Description: Length 33 inches (85 cm). Superficially similar to the Blue and Gold macaw, but can be easily distinguished by the throat markings: The throat patch is blue, as its common name implies, and the throat patch is considerably larger than the black patch of the previous species. Most of the upper body, including the wings and tail, are a light blue color, which in sunlight acquires a greenish tinge. Other than the throat, the underside of the body is light orange, as are the undertail coverts. The bare facial skin has several rows of fine blue feathers. The bill and legs are dull grayish black. The iris is yellow.

Distribution: The Blue-throated macaw has a very limited range that is restricted to the province of Beni, in eastern Bolivia.

Habitat and status: The wild population of the Blue-throated macaw has always been small numerically; today it is known that only around 100 birds remain in the wild. This makes the Blue-throated macaw the most endangered species in the wild from the genus of *Ara*. The wild population is confined to areas of forest islands and flooded lowlands in the Beni province of Bolivia. Fortunately, this species has become firmly established in captivity and an international studbook has been established to ensure that the captive population has the potential to be viewed as a conservation resource if required for restocking of the wild population at a future date. An active field conservation program has also been in place since the early 1990s to protect the remaining fragile wild population.

Personality: This species was practically unknown in captivity until the late 1970s; and the first captive breeding was achieved only as recently as 1984, since this time the Blue-throated macaw has gone on to be very successful at breeding in captivity. As a pet bird, it is extremely beautiful and has a quiet and pleasing personality, inquisitive but gentle. The highly

Blue and Gold macaw (Ara ararauna).

Blue-throated macaw (Ara glaucogularis).

endangered status of this species in the wild has meant that not until very recent years have young birds been available as potential hand-rearing pets. Previously, the price of young birds placed them beyond the potential of the pet market, but in North America during the past ten years breeding has become so prolific that young Blue-throated macaws can now be found offered for sale at prices not too different than for other species of larger macaws kept as pets.

Breeding: Although uncommon in aviculture until the 1980s on, the Blue-throated macaw has proved very successful at captive breeding. The clutch size is two to four eggs with incubation taking 26 days beginning soon after the first egg is laid. Parent-reared chicks will begin to fledge after 12 weeks of age. Hand-reared chicks may take longer to become independent.

Military Macaw
Ara militaris
CITES Appendix 1

Description: Length between 27 and 29 inches (70–75 cm). Most of the body is predominantly green; this color merges with blue toward the lower back, rump, and undertail coverts. The flight feathers are a greenish blue; the underside of the tail feathers is an olive green, and the upper side, a brownish red. The other noticeable coloration is the bright red band across the bird's forehead. The facial skin is bare apart from faint lines of black feathers running across it. The bill is dull gray, as are the legs. The iris is yellow. Three subspecies have been described.

Distribution: The three main populations are each regarded as distinct subspecies. The nominate subspecies *A. m. militaris* occurs from northwestern Venezuela to eastern Ecuador and northern Peru; *A. m. mexicana* is found throughout Mexico,

except in the rain forest zones; and *A. m. boliviana* inhabits the tropical zones of Bolivia and the northernmost region of Argentina.

Habitat and status: The Military macaw is known to occupy more open and exposed areas of habitat compared to other larger macaw species. In Mexico it can be found in semiarid, open countryside, although rarely too far away from water. It can also be found at much higher altitudes of up to 8,000 feet (2,500 m). The wild populations of all three subspecies appears stable, although their future depends upon appropriate land management across their ranges.

Personality: The Military macaw is well established in captivity, particularly in North America, although it has never shared the great popularity of the brighter-colored species of larger macaws. I find that even hand-reared birds of this species are generally moody and not completely trustworthy as pet birds unless handled very regularly by owners with time to spend consistently with the birds on a daily basis.

Breeding: Although not as popular, and therefore widely bred, as other larger more colorful species, the Military macaw has no doubt proved to be very successful as a subject for captive breeding. The clutch size is two to three eggs with incubation period of 26 days, which begins soon after the first egg is laid. Young chicks fledge after about 90 days when parent-reared; hand-reared birds take longer to become independent.

Buffon's Macaws
(also called the Great Green Macaw)
Ara ambigua
CITES Appendix 1

Description: Length 33 inches (85 cm). At first glance the Buffon's macaw is superficially similar to the previous species; however, the Buffon's macaw is noticeably larger; also, its plumage coloration is of a much lighter yellowish green. Most of the body is light green and turns blue around the lower back, rump, and undertail coverts. The forehead carries a broad scarlet band and the tail is red tipped, with blue above and olive yellow below. The facial skin is bare except for several fine lines of small black feathers. The bill is grayish black and becomes paler toward the tip. The legs are dark gray. The iris is yellow. Two subspecies of the Buffon's macaw are recognized, although there are only very slight visual differences between them.

Distribution: The Buffon's macaw has two main populations. The nominate subspecies, *A. a. ambigua,* is found through Central America from southeastern Honduras down to western Colombia; the second subspecies *A. a. guayaquilensis* is found in western Ecuador.

Habitat and status: The nominate subspecies of Buffon's macaws is recorded from areas of humid lowland forests. It is considered rare and declining across most of its range. A number of conservation program activities have been initiated in recent years. The subspecies *A. a. guayaquilensis* is restricted to a population of fewer than 100 birds and is highly endangered. An intensive conservation program is actively attempting to protect this fragile population.

Personality: The Buffon's macaw is a gentle giant among the macaw family. Although visually similar to the Military macaw, the personality of this slightly larger species is generally much softer and more open to a close pet-owner relationship. Prior to the mid-1990s the price of the Buffon's macaw placed this species outside of the pet market, but in the past few years, prolific breeding, particularly in North America, has seen hand-reared birds of this species being offered for sale at prices that allow them to now be considered as pet birds.

Breeding: The Buffon macaw has always been a rare bird in captivity with only a small captive population; only recently has captive breeding become successful enough for this species to be considered well established in captivity. Clutch size is between two and four eggs; incubation begins soon after the first egg has been laid and lasts for 26 days when parent-reared fledging takes place after the ninth week. Hand-reared chicks will require longer to become independent.

Red-fronted Macaw

(also called Red-cheeked or Lafresnaye's Macaw)
Ara rubrogenys
CITES Appendix 1

Description: Length 24 inches (60 cm). The main body plumage is olive green, which becomes brighter towards the head and shoulders. The forehead, crown, spot behind the eye, and thighs are red; the bend of the wing, lesser wing coverts, and underwing coverts are orange to red. The tail is olive green and tipped with blue above and olive yellow below. The facial area of bare skin is smaller compared to other species already mentioned, and is pinkish white in color. The bill is grayish black, as are the legs. The iris is orange.

Distribution: This species has a limited range within the country of Bolivia, confined mainly to the southern central region of the country.

Habitat and status: The Red-fronted macaw inhabits limited areas in arid, scrub-type regions below 8,000 feet (2,500 m) in altitude. The species is described as being locally common in

Military macaw (**Ara militaris**).

Buffon's macaw (**Ara ambigua**).

the limited range areas it inhabits. The total wild population is however considered to be fewer than 4,000 individuals.

Personality: The Red-fronted macaw is smaller than the previously described species and has good pet potential. Previously, the rareness of this species has meant that it commands a price beyond what would be reasonable for a pet bird. In recent years, however, consistent breeding has been increasingly achieved, meaning that today the Red-fronted macaw is available at prices that allow them to be considered as pets, despite the endangered status of this species in the wild. Hand-reared birds can become extremely tame and usually maintain a consistent personality.

Breeding: The Red-fronted macaw only became well established in aviculture from the 1980s on, but has bred very successfully and is today common in aviculture. The clutch consists of between two and four eggs, which are incubated for 26 days, starting soon after the first egg has been laid. Parent-reared chicks begin to fledge after 84 days of age on. Hand-reared chicks may require longer to become independent.

Severe Macaw
(also called Chestnut-fronted Macaw)
Ara severa
CITES Appendix II

Description: Length 19 inches (49 cm). The main plumage color is green, which becomes bluish over the top of the head. Bordering the bare facial area, some brown coloration runs down the sides of the cheeks and under the

Red-fronted macaw (**Ara rubrogenys**).

Severe macaw (**Ara severa**).

chin and also forms a band across the forehead. Chestnut brown coloration can be found on the tips of the breast feathers, giving this species its alternative common name. There is red on the outer primaries, bend of the wing, and carpal edge; red can be found on the underwing coverts, although most of the underwing is olive brown. The primary coverts on the upper wing are blue. The tail is reddish orange. The bare skin on the face is white and has fine black lines running across it. The bill is dark gray, as are the legs. The iris is yellow.

Distribution: Range is from eastern Panama to the Guianas, and from northeastern Brazil south to Bolivia.

Habitat and status: Known to prefer open forests, the Severe macaw inhabits primary and secondary forest areas, forest edges, and open

woodlands across its range. It is usually found at altitudes below 5,000 feet (1,500 m). This species is considered common across most of its range.

Personality: The Severe macaw has been established in aviculture for many years, but is perhaps commonly available only in North American aviculture. It is more uncommonly kept in Europe and hand-reared specimens are not easily accessible outside of North America. Pet potential of this species is good, where young hand-reared birds are available. The Severe macaw has proved a popular pet bird in North America. For a small psittacine, it has a strong voice compared to many other medium and small-sized parrot species.

Breeding: Breeding has been achieved widely in aviculture, but the strongest population of

Severe macaws has always been in North America. The clutch size is generally two to three eggs, which are incubated for 25 days beginning soon after the first egg has been laid. When parent-reared the young can spend as long as 12 weeks in the nest before fledging. Hand-reared chicks are usually weaned by 12 weeks.

Yellow-collared Macaw
(also called Yellow-naped Macaw)
Ara auricollis
CITES Appendix II

Description: Length 15 inches (38 cm). The main coloration over the body is green. The forehead, crown, and lower cheeks are brown. The species gets its common name from the yellow collar that extends around the hind neck. There is also some blue on the underwings, mainly on the primaries. The tail is blue and becomes reddish brown toward the base; the underside of the tail is yellow, as is the underside of the flight feathers. The bare facial skin is a creamy white color. The bill is dark gray, which becomes lighter toward the tip. The legs are pink. The iris is orange.

Distribution: The Yellow-collared macaw is found from northern and eastern regions of Bolivia, east into Brazil, and south into northern Paraguay to northwestern Argentina, also some isolated populations in central Brazil.

Habitat and status: This species inhabits a variety of differing habitats, such as humid forests, woodlands, and even agricultural lands. It is considered common and abundant in most areas across its range.

Personality: When available as young hand-reared birds, Yellow-collared macaws can make good pets. They have a pleasant personality and are lively and inquisitive. Their personality can become strong and regular, and consistent handling may be needed to keep such boisterous birds hand tame. Also, as with other macaw species, despite its smaller size the voice is loud.

Breeding: The Yellow-collared macaw has proved easy to breed in captivity and is considered one of the best "beginners" species to care for within the macaw family. The clutch size is usually two to four eggs, which are incubated for 25 days beginning soon after the first egg has been laid. When parent-reared the young will begin to fledge by the tenth week of age. Hand-reared birds should become independent at about the same age.

Red-bellied Macaw
Ara manilata
CITES Appendix II

Description: Length 20 inches (50 cm). The main plumage coloration is green, tinged with olive over the neck, back, rump, uppertail coverts, and lower underparts. The crown and the lower cheeks have a bluish tinge, as do the primaries and primary coverts in the wing and the underside of the tail feathers. The throat and breast feathers are gray, edged with green. A broad red patch covers the lower abdomen down to the vent and gives this bird its common name. The feathers of the thighs are also edged with red. The bare facial skin is yellow. The bill is grayish black, as are the legs. The iris is dark brown.

Distribution: This species ranges widely throughout northern South America. It is found from the Guianas, through northern and southeastern Venezuela to Colombia, then south to eastern Peru, northern Bolivia, and Brazil; also found on the island of Trinidad.

Habitat and status: The Red-bellied macaw is considered a bird of lowland humid forest, rarely found in more open exposed habitat.

Although its distribution is extensive, it is usually localized in areas of undisturbed forest across this range. The species is still regarded as locally common in undisturbed areas of habitat across its range.

Personality: The Red-bellied macaw does not generally make a good pet species. Breeding is less common in this species compared to other smaller macaws in aviculture and adult birds usually prove to be more difficult to manage over prolonged periods of time due to the species' selective feeding habits and extreme sensitivity toward obesity. The Red-bellied macaw appears to have a much more specialized diet in the wild, compared to other smaller macaw species, being highly dependent upon the fruits of Buriti palm trees. Not recommended as a pet species.

Breeding: The Red-bellied macaw is not well established in aviculture, but has been bred in several collections. I have bred this species successfully in two different zoological collections. The species generally does better when maintained on a low-fat diet with close attention to prevent obesity. This species also requires plenty of flying space to exercise and is considered more nervous in behavior than other smaller macaw species. Clutch size can be between two and five eggs, which are incubated for 25 days beginning soon after the first egg is laid. When parent-reared, young birds will begin to fledge by the eleventh week. Hand-reared birds become independent by about the same age.

Illiger's Macaw
Ara maracana
CITES Appendix I

Description: Length 17 inches (43 cm). Main plumage coloration is green, which becomes blue over the top of the head and cheeks. There is a bright red band across the forehead and another across the lower abdomen; the lower back is also red. These red patches make the species quite distinctive. The green of the rump area and uppertail coverts is tinged with olive. The primaries and primary coverts are blue, with some blue on the secondaries. The tail is blue above, becoming reddish toward the base; below is olive yellow. The bare facial skin is pale yellow. The bill is black. The legs are yellow; the iris is orange.

Distribution: Found widely within Brazil; also found south through Paraguay to northern Argentina.

Habitat and status: Reported to prefer primary forest, this species is also found more scarcely in open areas as well. Reported to be rare and declining across most of its range, eastern Brazil is considered to be its population stronghold. The wild population of Illiger's macaw has been placed on Appendix 1 of CITES since 1989, protecting it from commercial trade.

Personality: The Illiger's macaw has never been widely kept in aviculture and has not been considered as a pet species. Although the personality of this species is similar to that of other smaller macaws, and hand-reared birds can become very tame, the endangered status of this species combined with its scarce presence in aviculture have meant that its pet potential has not been seriously considered. With other more common small macaw species, such as the Severe macaw and Yellow-collared macaw, available to fill the same niche in the pet bird market, captive specimens of the Illiger's macaw are normally reserved for breeding stock.

Yellow-collared macaw (**Ara auricollis**).

Illiger's macaw (**Ara maracana**).

Breeding: Although rarer in aviculture than other smaller macaw species, it has been my experience that the Illiger's macaw breeds extremely well and prolifically in captivity. The clutch size is usually between three and five eggs, which are incubated for 25 days beginning soon after the first egg has been laid. Parent-reared chicks will begin to fledge by the tenth week of age; hand-reared chicks usually wean at around a similar age.

Blue-headed Macaw

(also called Coulon's Macaw)
Ara couloni
CITES Appendix I

Description: Length 16 inches (41 cm). The main plumage over the body is green, becoming slightly more yellowish on the underside of the body. All of the head, with the exception of the bare area of facial skin, is blue, giving the species its common name and making it very visually distinctive. There is also some blue coloration in the wings, mainly on the primaries and primary coverts. The tail is blue above and yellow below. The skin of the bare facial patch is gray; the bill is dark gray, becoming lighter toward the tip. The legs are light brown. The iris is yellow.

Distribution: Natural range includes Eastern Peru, southwestern Brazil, and northern Bolivia.

Habitat and status: The Blue-headed macaw is reported to prefer forest edges and open woodland, although this species is studied very little in the wild. The size and status of the wild population is unsure and the species has been almost unknown in aviculture outside

Hahn's macaw (**Ara n. nobilis**).

Noble macaw (**Ara n. cumanensis**).

of a few zoological collections in Europe and the Philippines. A captive-breeding program for this species has now been approved in North America and a captive population will soon be established here.

Personality: My experience suggests that the personality of this species is pleasant and that captive-bred specimens can be tamed easily. However, because this species is so rare in captivity, all captive birds are being considered as breeding stock. As a result, no captive specimens of the Blue-headed macaw have been kept as pet birds. It is unlikely that the captive population will grow sufficiently over the next few years to stock the pet market.

Breeding: The Blue-headed macaw has only very recently been seen in captive zoological collections and breeding is only now beginning. Early results achieved at Loro Parque in 1998 and elsewhere suggest that breeding biology is similar to other small macaw species. Clutch size appears to be two to four eggs, which are incubated for 25 days. Parent-reared chicks begin to fledge after about ten weeks of age.

Genus Diopsittaca

The Hahn's macaw (and the subspecies known as the Noble macaw) was previously included within the genus of *Ara* for many decades. Recent revisions within the last decade have now shown a consensus that this species would be better placed in its own monotypic genus of *Diopsittaca*.

Hahn's Macaw/Noble Macaw

(also called Red-shouldered Macaw)

Diopsittaca nobilis nobilis/Diopsittaca nobilis cumanensis

CITES Appendix II

Two distinct subspecies are recognized, which have significant differences in size and visual appearance. The nominate subspecies *(A. n. nobilis)* is known as the Hahn's macaw and is distinct from the second subspecies, known as the Noble macaw *(A. n. cumanensis)* by being smaller and having a black bill, as opposed to the pale cream colored upper mandible of the Noble macaw.

Description: Length for the Hahn's macaw *(A. n. nobilis)* is 12 inches (30 cm) and for the Noble macaw *(A. n. cumanensis)* is 13 inches (34 cm). The main body plumage is green, which becomes yellowish on the underside of the body. The forehead and forecrown are blue, as are the outer primaries on the upper wing. The bend of the wing and the underside of the wing are red, giving the bird its alternative common name. The underside of the flight feathers and tail are olive yellow. The bare patch of facial skin is white. The bill is completely black in the Hahn's macaw, whereas in the Noble macaw the upper mandible is creamy white. Legs are gray. The iris is dark orange.

Distribution: Ranges from the Guianas, eastern Venezuela, and southward to southern Brazil, southeastern Peru, and northern Bolivia.

Habitat and status: This species is reportedly common across most of its range, occupying a variety of different habitats. It is most commonly found, however, in lowland areas of open woodland and forest edges. Both subspecies appear to be common and widespread in the wild.

Personality: The Hahn's macaw is well established and very commonly bred in aviculture. The Noble macaw is also well established but is slightly less common and more expensive than the nominate subspecies. Hand-reared specimens of the Hahn's macaw are commonly offered in the pet market and make delightful pets. Extremely tame and playful, their voice is still loud compared to other small species of parrots. Hand-reared Noble macaws can also make tame pets when hand-reared birds are available.

Breeding: Both the Hahn's and Noble macaws breed extremely well in captivity, although the Hahn's is by far the more widely kept and bred subspecies. The clutch size is usually between two and five eggs, which are incubated for 24 days beginning soon after the first egg has been laid. Parent-reared chicks can begin to fledge from the eighth week on. Hand-reared chicks usually take slightly longer to become independent.

Genus Andorhynchus

The genus of *Andorhynchus* contains three species, although one of these, the Glaucous macaw, is considered probably extinct and unknown in captivity; it is therefore not included in the individual descriptions. All three species in the genus share the typical macaw shape and are among the largest members of the parrot family. The facial area is feathered, unlike the *Ara* species, although there is some bare skin bordering the lower mandible. Additionally, there is a prominent periophthalmic ring.

Hyacinthine Macaw

(also called Hyacinthe Macaw)
Andorhynchus hyacinthinus
CITES Appendix I

Description: Length 39 inches (100 cm). The entire body plumage is a rich violet color. The only contrasting color is the yellow periophthalmic ring that encircles the eye and borders the lower mandible. The bill is dark gray, as are the legs. The iris is dark brown.

Distribution: The main population is found in northern Brazil; smaller populations have also been recorded in eastern Bolivia and northern Paraguay.

Habitat and status: The Hyacinthine macaw's preferred habitat is secondary forest and open woodland. The wild population has declined rapidly since the 1980s and today the wild population is thought to number around 6,000 individuals or fewer. The main stronghold for the wild population is the Pantanal, with smaller populations also found elsewhere in Brazil.

Personality: The personality of tame Hyacinthine macaws is outstanding and unique. Despite the enormous strength of these birds and their potential for inflicting dangerous bites, the personality of tame Hyacinthine macaws can be among the most gentle of all parrot species. The imposing size of the Hyacinthine macaw, its striking coloration, and the extremely gentle personality of tame specimens have given this species a place in the pet market for those owners fortunate to be able to afford to buy and maintain these expensive, large, and destructive birds. The price of young hand-reared birds is high, due to their endangered status in the wild and because *Andorhynchus* macaws usually prove harder to breed in captivity than *Ara* species of macaw. Despite the endangered status of this species, several specialist avicultural collections have successfully concentrated upon the breeding of the Hyacinthine macaw. This has ensured that enough birds are being captive-bred to allow some birds to be sold into the pet market, while still producing enough birds to ensure a strong breeding population for the future. The price of captive-bred specimens and their demands for space and high-quality housing are the main factors that have restricted them to an elite place in the pet bird market.

Breeding: The Hyacinthine macaw has generally proved more difficult to breed successfully in captivity than the larger species of *Ara* macaws. This is due to a combination of factors: a more specialist dietary requirement, greater need for privacy and attention to mate selection, and the high price of these birds, which restricts the abilities of aviculturists to obtain a large group of birds for mate selection. However, breeding has been consistently achieved by a number of private owners and zoological collections that have dedicated time to concentrate upon breeding this species. The clutch size is usually between two and three eggs, which are incubated for up to 28 days. When parent-reared, chicks will begin to fledge from the fourteenth week of age on; hand-reared chicks can take significantly longer to become independent.

Lear's Macaw

Andorhynchus leari
CITES Appendix I

Description: Length 30 inches (75 cm). The Lear's macaw, except for its smaller size, closely resembles the Hyacinthine macaw. It has the

Hyacinthe macaw (**Andorhynchus hyacinthinus**).

macaw, but more timid. This may be due in part to the fact that few captive-bred specimens exist. But the Lear's macaw seems to be more communal and nervous compared to the generally outgoing nature of the Hyacinthine macaw. The Lear's macaw is unlikely to ever be considered a pet bird species.

Breeding: Little information exists about the captive breeding of the Lear's macaw. The only known information originates from the successful rearing of two chicks at Busch Zoological Gardens in the early 1980s.

Genus Cyanopsitta

The genus of *Cyanopsitta* is monotypic, containing only a single species—the Spix's macaw. Physically it resembles many of the smaller *Ara* species, but is of medium size with a graduated tail. It can easily be distinguished from any other macaw by its light blue plumage and feathered cheek patches. This species is also distinct from all other macaws by the bare skin around the eyes and lores, which is dark.

Spix's Macaw

(also called the Little Blue Macaw)
Cyanopsitta spixii
CITES Appendix I

Description: Length 22 inches (56 cm). Main plumage coloration is light blue, which becomes slightly darker over the back, wings, and underside of the tail. The head is a lighter shade of blue and its feathers are edged with light gray. The cheeks are covered with feathers but there is a dark gray patch of bare skin surrounding the eye and reaching over the lores toward the bill. The bill and legs are dark gray. The iris is yellow.

same deep blue coloration. Apart from its size, another difference is the larger area of bare yellow skin bordering the lower mandible.

Distribution: The range is restricted to a small area within northeastern Brazil.

Habitat and status: The Lear's macaw is extremely endangered in the wild. The wild population is thought to number below 200 individuals and is confined to one main breeding colony. A second, very small colony of 25 birds has also been reported in a separate area.

Personality: The personality of captive Lear's macaws is similar to that of the Hyacinthine

Spix's macaw (**Cyanopsitta spixii**).

Distribution: Formerly confined to a small area of Brazil, now considered to be extinct in the wild. The small captive population still provides hope for possible future reintroduction to be considered.

Habitat and status: Now considered extinct in the wild, a captive population of around 70 birds exists in aviculture.

Personality: The pet potential of this species has never been considered due to its extreme rarity. Captive specimens cared for by me generally have quiet, nervous personalities. Even if the fragile captive population continues to grow numerically in the future, this species is unlikely to ever be considered as a pet species. Most captive specimens belong to the government of Brazil and the top priority is to reestablish a wild population.

Breeding: This species is kept only in a small number of captive zoological collections; most have had only limited success. Two collections have, however, been very successful, one in Switzerland and the other in the Philippines. Clutch size is between two and five eggs, which are incubated for 26 days. When parent-reared, chicks begin to fledge after eight weeks.

Glossary

Ascarids: A group of round wormlike parasites common in captive Psittacines.

Aspiration: The accidental inhalation of food into the trachea, and possibly the lungs. This event can lead to bacterial infections of the lungs and requires immediate veterinary attention.

Aviculture: Keeping and breeding birds in captivity.

Aviculturist: A person who keeps and breeds captive birds as a pastime or hobby

Avitaminosis: Any disease caused by a lack of certain vitamins from the diet, such as avitiminosis A from a lack of vitamin A in the diet.

Bend of the Wing: Area along the front top of the wing, covered by lesser wing coverts.

Calibrator: An instrument used for taking detailed measurements of length.

Candling: Using an artificial light source to enable development inside the egg to be viewed.

Cere: The flesh area around the nostrils. It is covered by feathers in some species and is bare in others.

Crop: A thin walled area of the lower esophagus, which can swell to hold excess food until the stomach empties or can hold food until it is needed for feeding chicks by regurgitation.

Crown: Area around the center of the top of the head.

Dry Bulb: The measuring instrument of temperature in an incubator.

Embryo: Term used for the early stages of development.

Endoscope: Surgical instrument used by a veterinarian to examine the gonads of a bird to determine its gender (can also be called a laparoscope).

Endoscopy: Surgical procedure in which a veterinarian uses an endoscope to view the gonads of a bird and ascertain its gender (can also be called laparoscopy).

Feces: Waste matter from the gut, which exits the body via the large intestines and cloaca.

Feral: Term given to domestic species that have become established in wild populations.

Fledgling: A young bird that just fledged (left the nest).

Foreneck: Area above the breast and just below the throat.

Genus: A group of species sharing common physical characteristics that make them distinct from other groups of species.

Incubator: Mechanical container used for artificial incubation of eggs.

Initial Internal Pip: The moment the embryo starts to push up to and against the membrane between itself and the air sac within the egg.

Internal Pip: The moment the embryo breaks through the membrane between itself and the air sac within the egg.

Iris: The colored part of the eye.

Laparoscope: The surgical instrument that is used by a veterinarian when surgical sexing is undertaken to ascertain the sexual gender of a bird (can also be called an endoscope).

Laparoscopy: The procedure of using a laparoscope to examine the gonads of a bird in order to ascertain its gender (can also be called endoscopy).

Lateral: Term used to indicate something coming from, or being present on, the side.

Lores: The area between the eye and the bill.

Mandible: The two parts (upper and lower) of the bill.

Mantle: The area between the hindneck and the shoulders, down to the upper back.

Mites: Small arachnid parasites that can infest captive populations of birds.

Monomorphic: Term given to birds when there are no easily identifiable visual differences between the males and females of that species.

Nape: The area at the back of the neck.

Necrotic: Describes areas of dead skin tissue present in a live animal.

Nominate: Term that is given to the first sub-species (race) of a full species to be described, from which all later variants are described as subspecies thereof.

Nuchal: Term sometimes used for the area between the nape and hindneck.

Occiput: Name of the area toward the back of the upper head just above the nape.

Pip: The moment when the chick first breaks through the shell of the egg prior to hatching.

Primaries: The outside ten flight feathers that give the bird its main flying power.

Psittacine: A bird from the psittaciformes order that includes all parrots and parrotlike species.

Quarantine: A period of isolation to ensure that a bird is not carrying an infectious disease.

Race: Old-fashioned term used to describe a subspecies.

Rump: Area above the base of the tail.

Scapulars: Feathers running down the back against the inner edge of the wing.

Secondaries: The inner ten flight feathers.

Sexual Dimorphism: Term relating to a noticeable visual difference between the genders of a species.

Species: Term used for a distinct subordinate of a genus.

Vent: The external area of the anus.

Weaning: The period when a young bird being reared begins to feed by itself until the time when the bird is feeding independently.

Wet Bulb: The instrument used in determining the exact level of humidity inside an incubator.

Useful Addresses

Association

Association of Avian Veterinarians
P.O. Box 811720
Boca Raton, FL 33481-1720
(561) 393-8901
Fax (561) 393-8902
www.aav.org

Organizations

For those interested in helping the conservation efforts being made to protect macaws in the wild, the following organizations may prove to be of interest and should be supported.

World Parrot Trust
c/o Paradise Park,
Hayle, Cornwall TR27 4HY
U.K.

Loro Parque Foundation
38400 Puerto de la Cruz
Tenerife, Canary Islands
Spain

Birdlife International
Wellbrook Court
Girton Road
Cambridge BC3 0NA
U.K.

American Bird Conservatory
1250 24th Street
NW, Suite 400
Washington, DC 20037

Avicultural Magazines

Bird Talk Magazine
P.O. Box 6050
Mission Viejo, CA 92690

Toys can help keep a macaw entertained and prevent behavioral problems.

Bird Times
7-L Dundas Circle
Greensboro, NC 27407

AFA Watchbird
American Federation of Aviculture
P.O. Box 56218
Phoenix, AZ 85079-6218

Cage and Aviary Birds
I.P.C. Magazines
Kings Reach Tower
Stamford Street
London SE1 9LS
U.K.

Birdkeeper Magazine
I.P.C. Magazines
Kings Reach Tower
Stamford Street
London SE1 9LS
U.K.

Magazine of the Avicultural Society
c/o Bristol Zoo
Clifton, Bristol
U.K.

Magazine of the Parrot Society
108b Fenlake Road
Bedford MK42 0EU
U.K.

Avicultural Societies

American Federation for Aviculture
P.O. Box 7312
N. Kansas City, MO 64116
www.afa.birds.org

International Avicultural Society
P.O. Box 2232
La Belle, FL 33975

Parrot Society of the United Kingdom
108b Fenlake Road
Bedford MK42 0EU
U.K.

The Avicultural Society
c/o Bristol Zoo
Clifton, Bristol
U.K.

The Parrot Society of New Zealand
P.O. Box 79-202
Royal Heights
Auckland
New Zealand

Australian Avicultural Society
P.O. Box 75
Salisbury
Queensland 4107
Australia

Manufacturers of Macaw Food Products

Kaytee Product Inc.
Attn: Customer Service
521 Clay Street, P.O. Box 230
Chilton, WI 53014
www.kaytee.com

Pretty Bird International, Inc.
5810 Stacy Trail / P.O. Box 177
Stacy, MN 55079-0177
Tel: 1-800-356-5020/Fax: 1-651-462-1844
www.prettybird.com

Assorted foods can be included into the design of toys to keep the macaw entertained.

Rolf C. Hagen Inc.
Canada
www.hagen.com

World's Largest On-line Parrot Information Link Page

www.aviancompanions.com/links/mare.html

About the Author

Roger G. Sweeney has been working with macaws for more than fifteen years. He has extensive experience in the management and breeding of macaws in captivity, ranging from the common pet species to the highly endangered Spix's and Hyacinthe macaw. He has worked as curator of birds in the world's most famous zoological collection of parrots: Loro Parque Foundation in the Canary Islands. Today he serves as Associate Director of the Graeme Hall Bird Sanctuary in Barbados.

Photo Credits

Joan Balzarini: pages 8 (left, right), 9, 16, 17, 20, 24 (top left, top right), 25 (left, right), 28, 36 (top right), 37 (top right), 40, 41, 45, 49, 52, 61, 65, 68, 69, 73, 76 (right), 77 (top, bottom), 84 (left, right), 85 (right), 92, 93; Norvia Behling: pages 24 (bottom), 44 (all), 56; Susan Green: pages 32, 33, 36 (top left), 37 (bottom); Robert and Eunice Pearcy: pages 3, 12, 48, 60, 81 (left, right), 85 (left); Robert G. Sweeney: page 89; B. Everett Webb: pages 5, 13, 21, 29, 36 (bottom left, bottom right), 37 (top left), 64, 72, 76 (left), 80 (left, right), 88

Cover Photos

Joan Balzarini

All inquiries should be addressed to:
Barron's Educational Series, Inc.
250 Wireless Boulevard
Hauppauge, NY 11788
http://www.barronseduc.com

Library of Congress Catalog Card No. 2002020571

Library of Congress Cataloging-in-Publication Data
Sweeney, Roger G.
    Macaws : a complete pet owner's manual / Roger G. Sweeney.—2nd ed.
        p. cm.
    Includes bibliographical references (p.).
    ISBN-13: 978-0-7641-1920-0
    ISBN-10: 0-7641-1920-6
    ⸰1. Macaws. I. Title.

SF473.M33 S94 2002
636.6'865—dc21   2002020571

Printed in China
19 18 17 16 15 14

Important Note

People who suffer from allergies to feathers or any kind of feather dust should not keep macaws. In case of doubt, check with the doctor before you acquire one.

In dealing with macaws, one may receive injuries from bites or scratches. Have such wounds attended to by a doctor. Although psittacosis (parrot fever) is not among the commonly seen illnesses of macaws (see page 53), it can produce symptoms in both humans and parrots that may be life-threatening. At any sign of a cold or flu, see a doctor immediately.